Apples
and
Oranges

Rabbi David S. Lieb

 TORAH AURA PRODUCTIONS

ISBN 10: 1-934527-09-2
ISBN 13: 978-1-934527-09-2

Torah Aura Productions • 4423 Fruitland Avenue, Los Angeles, CA 90058
(800) BE-Torah • (800) 238-6724 • (323) 585-7312 • fax (323) 585-0327
E-MAIL <misrad@torahaura.com> • Visit the Torah Aura website at www.torahaura.com

MANUFACTURED IN HONG KONG

For Our Grandchildren

Leah Rebecca Knobel   *Maxine Desmond Lieb*

Alana Michelle Knobel   *Sadie Jane Lieb*

ॐ

*May the Peoples of Their World Have Faith
and Trust in One Another and a Shared
Peace in God's Presence*

ॐ

Estelle and David Lieb

Rabbi David Lieb, 1942–2008

My brother, David Samuel Lieb, rabbi, husband, father, grandpa, brother, friend, author and lover of all things Jewish, loved life and was very good at it. His professional career included 34 consecutive years at Temple Beth El in San Pedro, California and a two year stint as a chaplain in the Army immediately following his ordination from Hebrew Union College in 1969. His understanding of all things spiritual stemmed from many things, especially his abiding faith in the Chicago Cubs and in the improvement of his mediocre golf game. The same optimism that led him to persist in these seemingly hopeless tasks made him a true believer in the goodness that is available in all of us.

David was a respected leader in San Pedro among his rabbinic colleagues and within the Reform movement. He chaired committees and consulted with task forces. But he saved special dedication for his congregants at Beth El and for his family, who miss him very much.

An avid joker and storyteller, he was an astonishing listener as well. It is not a surprise that the book that he finished at the end of his too-short life was to explain to all of us in as clear a way as possible how others celebrate their faith communities. David was deeply respectful, deeply intelligent, and deeply loving. This book is dedicated to that vision that was David's, to David who laughed large and loved with every ounce of his heart, and who wished the world could do that as well.

—Marilyn Jean Lieb Price

Contents

Chapter 1.
How to Compare Religions

What is Religion?

Here are a whole bunch of different (many famous) people's statements of what religion is. With a partner, read through these quotations and mark the ones you like, the ones you hate, and the one that seems most true to you.

_____ A religious man is a person who holds God and man in one thought at one time, at all times, who suffers harm done to others, whose greatest passion is compassion, whose greatest strength is love and defiance of despair. [New York *Journal-American*, April 5, 1963]—**Abraham Joshua Heschel**

_____ When I do good, I feel good; when I do bad, I feel bad. That's my religion.—**Abraham Lincoln**

_____ What do I believe? As an American I believe in generosity, in liberty, in the rights of man. These are social and political faiths that are part of me, as they are, I suppose, part of all of us. Such beliefs are easy to express. But part of me too is my relation to all life, my religion. And this is not so easy to talk about. Religious experience is highly intimate and, for me, ready words are not at hand. [Speech, Libertyville, Illinois, May 21, 1954]—**Adlai E. Stevenson**

_____ The most beautiful emotion we can experience is the mysterious. It is the fundamental emotion that stands at the cradle of true art and science. He to whom this emotion is a stranger, who can no longer wonder and stand in awe, is as good as dead, a snuffed-out candle. To sense that beyond anything that can be experienced there is something that our minds cannot grasp, whose beauty and sublimity reaches us only indirectly; this is religiousness. In this sense, and in this sense only, I am a devoutly religious man.—**Albert Einstein**

_____ Religion is what an individual does with his solitariness.—**Alfred North Whitehead**

_____ The best remedy for those who are afraid, lonely or unhappy is to go outside, somewhere where they can be quiet, alone with the heavens, nature and God. Because only then does one feel that all is as it should be and that God wishes to see people happy, amidst the simple beauty of nature.—**Anne Frank**

_____ Lighthouses are more helpful than churches.—**Benjamin Franklin**

_____Religion is the everlasting dialogue between humanity and God.— **Franz Werfel**

_____ There is a marvelous anecdote from the occasion of Russell's ninetieth birthday that best serves to summarize his attitude toward God and religion. A London lady sat next to him at this party, and over the soup she suggested to him that he was not only the world's most famous atheist but, by this time, very probably the world's oldest atheist. "What will you do, Bertie, if it turns out you're wrong?" she asked. "I mean, what if—uh—when the time comes, you should meet God? What will you say?" Russell was delighted with the question. His bright, birdlike eyes grew even brighter as he contemplated this possible future dialogue, and then he pointed a finger upward and cried, "Why, I should say, 'God, you gave us insufficient evidence.'"—**Al Seckel**, in Preface to _Bertrand Russell on God and Religion_]

_____ Let us revere, let us worship, but erect and open-eyed, the highest, not the lowest; the future, not the past!—**Charlotte Perkins Gilman**

_____ Religion is the supreme art of humanity.—**Abba Hillel Silver**

_____ I do not consider it an insult, but rather a compliment to be called an agnostic. I do not pretend to know where many ignorant men are sure—that is all that agnosticism means. [Scopes trial, Dayton, Tennessee, July 13, 1925]—**Clarence Darrow**

_____ This is my simple religion. There is no need for temples; no need for complicated philosophy. Our own brain, our own heart is our temple; the philosophy is kindness.—**The Dalai Lama**

_____ All human beings have an innate need to hear and tell stories and to have a story to live by…religion, whatever else it has done, has provided one of the main ways of meeting this abiding need. [_The Seduction of the Spirit_, 1973]—**Harvey Cox**

_____ Religion is the recognition of all our duties as divine commands.—**Immanuel Kant**

_____ Religion is the state of being grasped by an ultimate concern, a concern which qualifies all other concerns as preliminary and which itself contains the answer to the question of the meaning of our life.—**Paul Tillich**

_____ One man's religion is another man's belly laugh.—**Robert A. Heinlein**

_____ I think it's about time we gave up religion and got back to God.—**Lenny Bruce**

_____ People don't come to church for preachments, of course, but to daydream about God.—**Kurt Vonnegut, Jr.**

_____ I considered atheism, but there weren't enough holidays.—**Author Unknown**

_____ Religion is the sigh of the oppressed creature, the heart of a heartless world, just as it is the spirit of a spiritless situation. It is the opiate of the people.—**Karl Marx**

_____ Religion is the human attitude towards a sacred order that includes within it all being—human or otherwise—i.e., belief in a cosmos, the meaning of which both includes and transcends man.—**Peter Berger**

_____ Religion: Human beings' relation to that which they regard as holy, sacred, spiritual, or divine.—*Encyclopædia Britannica* **(online, 2006)**

_____ To be religious is to have one's **attention** fixed on God and on one's neighbor in relation to God. ["Lilies that Fester" in *The Twentieth Century* (April 1955)]—**C.S. Lewis**

_____ Religion is to do right. It is to love, it is to serve, it is to think, it is to be humble.—**Ralph Waldo Emerson**

_____ Religion is man's conviction that there is a power other than himself, creatively and constantly driving him onward and upward to undreamed of heights of hope and happiness. Religion is man's most venturesome and dramatic act of faith--an attempt to attain and understand the secret of God.—**Louis Binstock**

_____ True religion shoes its influence in every part of our conduct; it is like the sap of a living tree which pentrates the most distant boughs.— **Robert A Rothman**

Apples and Oranges

Everybody knows you can't compare apples and oranges; it's so commonly understood that we use that expression even when we're not talking about apples and oranges. Yet apples and oranges share many qualities about which we can make certain comparative statements: they are both fruits, they are both round, they both

have color and flavor, they both can be made into juice and they both have seeds. Some people like apples more than they like oranges and vice versa, and there are times in our day when we feel more like eating an apple than we do an orange. (For instance, I would never have an apple at breakfast time; to me it just isn't a breakfast kind of fruit. But I might eat an orange at almost any time of day.)

The business of comparing things that are so apparently different becomes even more complicated and subtle when we leave behind the world of fruit and enter the world of religion. Just about everybody knows what a fruit is (although I'm not so sure about tomatoes), but religion and particular religions take us to a whole different level of investigation and discussion. Just as it is actually correct that you can compare oranges and apples, so it is that you can compare religions. But as with fruit, it would be better to think beyond surface appearances, ask deeper and more careful questions and truly appreciate the complicated realities that give religions their individual appearances and flavors.

At this early point, what do you think a religion is? What defines the key parts of Judaism as you know it now? How is a religion different from a culture?

Now, since everybody knows what a fruit is (except for me with tomatoes), let's see if everybody knows what a religion is. Apples and oranges are both fruits, and despite many obvious dissimilarities, they both fall into the fruit department at the supermarket. They share "fruitiness". But what defines the essential character of all of those things we call "religion" that it will be our business to compare with one another? What are the basic elements that make up what we call a religion?

10

What Is Religion?

Someone once taught that the origin of the word "religion" is from the Greek and Latin roots of the word "ligament," the connective tissue that binds together our skeletal structure. Even if the word's history is difficult to trace exactly, and even if it applies only to those languages that came from Greek and Latin, it still seems like a really good idea. Religion is the "connective tissue" that binds together the skeletal structure of a particular body—in particular, the "body" of a community of people who share and believe in certain ideas about certain things, and who have had shared experiences involving those shared ideas. A **religious community** is a community that has shared beliefs about certain kinds of issues that are important to them.

But as we usually understand religion, those shared beliefs are not just about any old thing or any kind of experience. Those shared beliefs (or values or perspectives) are about certain kinds of subjects that throughout human history have been understood as "religion". There may be other ideas and experiences that bind a community together in a different kind of way. For example, people from the north side of Chicago are bound together by the beliefs and experiences that come from the miserable failure of the Chicago Cubs to win a World Series since 1908. People in France or China or Brazil are bound together by language, culture, art and music. A community can be tied together by many factors, and we live in many separate communities—school, friends, family—that bind us as well. Our religious community is the community that binds us with those shared ideas we have come to call "religion." Let's see what they are.

11

REVELATION is more or less understood to mean a variety of experiences in which God is revealed, either by God's own initiative or through the discovery of God's Presence by some human being. Some of these moments are quite dramatic, some are very simple and quiet.

Perhaps the most famous such moment in Jewish tradition is the revelation at Mt. Sinai, recorded in Chapters 19 and 20 of the Book of Exodus. How does this story emphasize the authority of God and Moses? What is being revealed here? Is there anything you can discover about the nature of the Jewish God in this story? What exactly is God hoping to accomplish here? Why is it important that this story is taking place when it does? What does it mean to have faith (to believe) in the power of this moment, what it says and what it asks us to do? How are the Ten Commandments both personal and institutional? That ought to keep you busy for a while!

You might also take a look at Exodus 34, in which God speaks directly to Moses and we learn much about the nature of God. In many ways this is a more personal revelation meant to help Moses out, but it also says some important things for all Jews to think about. What are some of those ideas?

The Basic Elements of Religion (I Think)

Obviously (I hope), one of those ideas is what we think about **GOD** and **FAITH**. We may use many different vocabularies to talk about God. Words like "sacred", "divine", and "holy" are all words in English that have to do with God or what religious people perceive as God's presence or involvement. There are times when we use these words in non-religious contexts—e.g., the sacred game of baseball—but in general, when a religious group uses these words they are talking about all of the different issues that define what they think about God. When we compare religions, we need to compare the different or similar ideas that communities have about the nature of God. And sometimes, to use an old friend, we just might be talking about apples and oranges!

When communities talk about their ideas of God, they are also often talking about another important issue for our comparisons. They are talking about the issue of **AUTHORITY** and **LEADERSHIP**. In religions, authority is a big deal, and it's one of those things we have to understand in order to be clear about what makes religions the same or different. At a simple level, of course, authority is about who's in charge (or Who's in charge.) It's related to God because in most of human religious experience, the authority is either God directly or whoever it is that can successfully claim to speak for God or interpret what it is that God has to say. Most religions call that **REVELATION**, and most religions teach about one or several of those kinds of experiences (revelations) in which they believe God made known to them what's really important.

Another very interesting question arises when you look at the word "authority" and realize that it has something to do with an "author".

Both words trace back to the Latin root *auctoritatum*. Let's hear you use that in a sentence.

Most religious communities have a basic text, written somewhere in the beginning, telling the stories and values that shape their ideas and identities. Judaism has the Torah, Christianity has the

"Christian Scriptures", Islam has the Qu'ran and each of the many Eastern religions has a basic text as well. For each of them, the authorship of this primary text is a critical question that tells us much about the nature of the community. If God wrote or revealed the "book" and gave it to the community, it cannot easily be changed or ignored by mere humans. But if the book is, for example, the story of one person's encounter with God, perhaps the book can be amended based on experiences that someone else in the community has had. (This is as much a critical issue for comparative Judaism as it is for comparative religions.)

In Judaism there are some very beautiful stories about the "writing" of the Torah given to Moses. The Ten Commandments story is followed by Moses' return to Sinai to get the rest of the Laws. The Rabbis composed several *midrashim* (story-sermons) about that more complete Torah. One story says it was written with black fire; another says that God actually dictated it to Moses to write down. There are stories that say that the Torah pre-dated the creation of the world, and that God used it as the blueprint for how the world was going to be.

© PAIGE BILLIN FRYE

Also related to questions about God and authority are questions about leadership within the community. Rabbis, priests, teachers, pastors, imams and mullahs all reflect different ideas about the nature of leadership. Some communities like the Mormons have no clergy; many religions emphasize the absolute autonomy (free choice) of the individual to interpret religious ideas all by herself or himself. How religions structure themselves is a very important issue for our comparative studies.

Speaking of the stories that tell of the beginning of a community and its beliefs (whoever wrote those stories), almost all religious communities have a continuing and growing body of such stories. These later stories contribute to the "connective tissue," often making it stronger and more lasting. Jewish history is a particularly clear example of this phenomenon. Though we began with the stories of the Torah, just think of what later stories (such as Hanukkah, the Holocaust and the rebirth of Israel) have added to our "ligaments". In fact, one could easily say that new beliefs and values have entered the Jewish soul and changed the body of our people. The encounter with the modern world gave birth to Reform, Conservative and Reconstructionist Judaism, and one could argue that they are new religious communities all their own. In many ways this process has also happened to other religions, and how religions adapt to change and new ideas (or don't) is part of what we ought to compare about them.

The **CELEBRATION** of those stories, in all religions, is what gives birth to many of our rituals and holidays. If religions didn't

have those expressions, they might not so easily remember who they are. If we wish to understand why a religion looks as it does, we need to see the connections between their rituals and their stories in the same way that you and I understand why we eat latkes at Hanukkah. For many students of comparative religions, this is the fun part, for if nothing else, it at least involves the possibility of something to eat.

There are yet other beliefs or values that seem to appear in almost all religious communities, although in varying degrees of importance. This is the issue of **SALVATION**, and a question it often raises about our interaction with the rest of the world and its challenges. In many ways, these two questions are part of the big question that people think religions are supposed to deal with: **WHAT IS THE MEANING OF LIFE**? Salvation means "to be saved," and in the religion business, the big salvation question is, What are we going to be saved from? For many religions the answer is death, and in those religions there are serious teachings about how a person is saved from all that it means to die. In many other religions, the answer is injustice and how we are to be saved (or how we are to save others) from what is an unfair and cruel world. And for many religions the answer is that we need to find a way in which we are saved from both death and injustice. As we compare religious communities we will want to know what things they think we need to find salvation from and how they propose we find it. And sometimes, as I hope you will see, religious teachings can be a little vague about these questions because they're not sure anybody knows! But these are big questions that may take us to the very serious center of religious life.

Finally, we should say in our list of the elements of religion that most of the time, as a product of the first four, religions will produce a list of their **CORE VALUES**. This means that when you carefully analyze what a religion teaches you should be able to develop some idea of those things that are at the center (core) of what they value, and you should be able to trace each of those values to one of the other four elements. It's not always easy or direct, and we may not have enough information to do that in every case, but I hope your class will give it a try.

◆ ◆ ◆

Finally, to return to apples and oranges for a moment, within the collection of beliefs and values that define each religion there are probably going to be some that aren't universally shared or that are unique to a given community. We might enjoy knowing about them in order to understand that community more fully, but there may not be any basis for comparison other than to say, "Nobody else does that." If we were professional historians or theologians (people who study religion for a living), we might like to know why this community did that, but it may not be what we'll do now.

So you now have a better understanding of what religion is and what the issues are that define most, if not all, religions and can help us see the signposts for comparison. Talk among yourselves for a while, and then we'll get to work.

The Elements of Religion

"Minds do not **create** truths or falsehood. They create beliefs, but when once the beliefs are created, the mind cannot make them true or false, except in the special case where they concern future things which are within the power of the person believing, such as catching trains. What makes a belief true is a **fact**, and this fact does not (except in exceptional cases) in any way involve the mind of the person who has the belief." (Bertrand Russell, *The Problems of Philosophy*)

1. What is the difference between a belief and a truth or falsehood? _____

   _____

   _____

   _____

2. What does Russell mean when he says "the mind cannot make beliefs true or false"?

   _____

   _____

   _____

3. According to Russell, what makes a belief true? _____

   _____

   _____

4. How would Russell explain religion? _____

   _____

   _____

   _____

Creating a Religion

Make up your own religion. Filling the following categories:

1. **GOD AND FAITH** (Who is the God, and what are you supposed to believe?)

   _____

   _____

   _____

2. **AUTHORITY AND LEADERSHIP** (Who are the leaders of this religion, and what authority do they have? How did they get that authority?)

   _____

   _____

   _____

3. **REVELATION** (How does God communicate with people?)

   _____

   _____

   _____

4. **CELEBRATION** (What are the major holidays? Why and how are they celebrated?)

   _____

   _____

   _____

5. **SALVATION** (What is "saved," and how do you get there?)

   _____

   _____

   _____

6. **THE MEANING OF LIFE** (What is the purpose of living?)

_____

_____

_____

7. **CORE VALUES** (What are this religion's most important values?)

_____

_____

_____

Chapter 2.
Some Important and Unique Things to Remember About Judaism

Hebrew School Equivalency Exam

Before we study a chapter on Judaism, let's find out how much of the "nothing" you've studied during your Jewish education you've recalled.

Couples Quiz

Match these husbands and wives (2 points each).

Abraham	Rebekkah
Isaac	Sarah
Jacob	Bathsheva
King David	Zipporah
Moses	Hannah
Solomon	Haggar
Adam	Rachel
Elkanah	Eve
	Queen of Sheba
	Leah

Ordering Holidays

Put these Jewish holidays in the order in which they come in a Jewish year. Make Passover number 1 (2 points each).

_____ Rosh ha-Shanah

_____ Passover

_____ Hanukkah

_____ Sukkot

_____ Shavuot

_____ Simhat Torah

_____ Purim

_____ Yom Ha-Atzmaut

_____ Yom Kippur

_____ Tisha B'av

A Sense of Jewish History

Match the person and the period (1 point each).

Rachel	Hasidic Movement
Deborah	Holocaust
Saul	Judges
Ezra	Founding of the State of Israel
Rabbi Akiva	Kings
Maimonides	Babylonian Exile (Return)
Baal Shem Tov	Talmudic
Emma Lazarus	Golden Age of Spain
Hannah Senesh	Patriarchs and Matriarchs
Ben Gurion	Immigration to America

Best possible score is 50 points.

Basic Judaism 101

© TAMIR ORBAUM

Before we go on to examine and compare Judaism to the other great religions of the world, it might be a good thing to remind ourselves of its basic ideas and beliefs. Many educators will tell us that we can learn a great deal about a subject by comparing it to similar subjects; for example, one of the best ways to learn

A TIMELIME OF JEWISH HISTORY

BEFORE THE COMMON ERA (B.C.E.)

18th century:
Age of the Patriachs

1280: Exodus from Egypt

1240: Conquest of Canaan

1004-965: King David

586: Destruction of Jerusalem by the Babylonians

70-year exile to Babylonia begins

444: Ezra reads the Torah in Jerusalem

332: Alexander the Great conquers Jerusalem

164: Judah Maccabee recaptures the Temple from Antiochus IV (Hanukkah)

63: Rome conquers Jerusalem

DURING THE COMMON ERA (C.E.)

70: Romans destroy Jerusalem; beginning of Diaspora

73: Fall of Masada

200: Talmudic Academy established in Babylonia

480: Talmud completed

638: Arabs conquer Jerusalem

1099: Jerusalem conquered by Crusaders

1135: Maimonides born

1480: Inquisition established in Spain

1492: Jews expelled from Spain

1550: Kabbalah prominent in Israel and elsewhere

1654: First Jews arrive in America

1818: First Reform synagogue consecrated in Hamburg, Germany

1882: First Aliyah (of five major settlements) to Israel

1933: Hitler rises in Germany; Holocaust follows

1948: Establishment of the State of Israel

more about English is to study another language. That's certainly true, but we can also save a lot of time and energy if we can read about that other language in English! In the same way, as we compare Judaism with other religions we'll save a lot of time and energy if we look at them through our Jewish eyes and through what we know (and value) about being Jewish. So in this lesson we'll reinforce our Basic Judaism 101 before we meet everybody else's 101.

Judaism is one of the oldest surviving religious expressions in the history of human civilization.

Judaism has gone through a tremendous number of changes, additions and subtractions, and reinterpretations. It has been splintered (into what we most often call denominations), and it has had some of the widest differences of opinion of any religious expression. As a result, it is very difficult to come up with a simple definition that manages to answer the question "Just what is Judaism anyway?"

In twenty-five words or less (a lot less), it is probably most correct, and will certainly get you in a lot less trouble, if you define Judaism as "the religious expression of the Jewish people". In even more words, Judaism is what Jewish people do when they want to experience and talk about and celebrate all of the different ideas we discussed in our first lesson. Now, that doesn't tell you anything about the substance of Judaism—i.e., what those beliefs and values and behaviors might be—but it does tell you that Judaism, more than any other religion, is uniquely tied to the experiences of one particular group of people. If you are a follower of Judaism, it is because you are a Jewish person. When a Jewish person wants to talk about God ideas, he or she is all of a sudden involved with Judaism, because Judaism is what Jews do when they do religious things. If you convert to Judaism, you become a member of the Jewish people.

Or to put it another way, if you're a Jew (your people), you practice Judaism as your religion, if you do religion. If you practice Judaism, Jews are your people. And even though there are Jewish people who will say that they do not believe or do not wish to practice all of those beliefs and values and behaviors, it remains the case that only Jews do Judaism, and vice versa. So now it is our task to review what it is that Jews have taught and believed about

How would you describe what Judaism is? Your answer might include the religious "ism" born in the land of Judah, the way the people Israel lives out their covenant with God, the collective wisdom of Jewish history and experience, a collection of ideas and behaviors and traditions, etc.

those things that our last lesson told us were the great religious things human beings do.

◆ ◆ ◆ ◆

GOD: A recent study produced a list of 109 different names that Jewish history has used for God. This list was developed from the Bible, Rabbinic texts, traditional and new prayers—all of the sources where one could expect to find what it is that Jewish people think about when they think about God. Based on this list and many other things, one could conclude that there is no one Jewish idea that defines the One.

I am Who I am	I will be Who I will be	Adonai, "Eternal"
God	The Divinity, Divine One	Mighty One of Jacob Most High God
Almighty God of the Covenant	Everlasting Rock	Everlasting Arms
God of Hosts	Holy One	Shepherd of Israel
Ruler of Israel	Former of All	Guardian of Israel
Rock of Israel	Ruler	The True God
The Fear of Isaac	El, the God of Israel	Everlasting God
Ancient God	Everlasting Life	Creator of Heaven and Earth
Holy One of Israel	The Rock	The God of Truth
Praiseworthy God	Shield of Abraham	Ruler of Rulers
The Name	Heaven	The Awesome One
Eternal One of Israel	The Redeemer	Our God, God of our Ancestors
God of Abraham	God of Isaac	God of Jacob
God of Sarah	The Mighty One	Acquirer of All
Rescuer	Parent of Mercy	Merciful One
The Place	The Faithful One	The One Who Spoke and the Universe Came into Being
The Infinite	Hosts	Rock of Our Lives
"Thankworthy" God	Master of All	Our Shepherd
Our Healer	The Living God of Majesty	The Compassionate One
The Merciful One	The Bountiful One	The Most High
The Holy One Who Is to Be Praised	Peace	Judge of the Earth
My Rock	Ever-living God	The Ransomer
The Guide	The Heroic One	The Living God
Reviver of the Dead	The Merciful One	The Holy God
The Might	God of the Universe	The Possessor of Will

Ruler of Compassion and Mercy	Master of the Universe	Maker of Peace
The Holy Ruler	The Good One	Mighty One of Israel
Our Parent	The Creator	Mentor
Sovereign	Our Ruler	The One Who Is Forgiveness
The Generous One	The Patient One	The First Cause
Absolute Spirit	Hidden of Hiddens	The Eternal
Ancient of Ancients	The Power That Makes for Salvation	Absolute Rest
The Power That Makes for the Fulfillment of All Valid Ideals	World Soul	Shehinah (means the indwelling presence of God)
Source of Life		
Source of Peace	The One Whose Face Is Hidden	Keeper of Peace
	Yah (a biblical name for God, as in	

But if you examine the long history of Jewish thought about God, there are certain constants that distinguish what Jews who believe in God believe. First and foremost, as you may have studied, there is but One. Needless to say, we have disagreed about what even so simple an idea as that may mean. For example, the great philosopher Maimonidies taught the "oneness" of God meant that God was indivisible, unified, so that it was not appropriate to talk about different aspects of the Divine Being like justice and goodness. But then again, he was a philosopher, and you know how they are!

For most of history the ideas that have dominated the Jewish discussion of Godliness have been about three big things: **creation,** the **revealing** of the Torah, and **redemption or salvation**, what it means for Jewish people to be "saved" and from what they are saved. A fourth big idea we must add is the special **covenantal relationship** between God and the people Israel, the idea that we have a unique covenant or partnership with God that nobody else has. Jews who are serious about religion deal with these ideas, and though there are disagreements about how these ideas work themselves out, they are the big things that concern us about the Big Thing.

What you may have noticed is that these primary ideas (creation, revelation, redemption and covenant) are more about our **relationship** with God than about what God **is**. Because we are somehow created in the image of God, because the Jewish people have a covenant with God, because we were all present at the Exodus from Egypt and the revelation at Sinai *(Didn't I see you there?)*, Judaism is very explicit about our responsibility to bring holiness into our lives and the lives of our various communities.

So you could say that God **is** the Presence in our lives and our world that motivates us to behave in ways that make an important difference. As the Rabbis teach, "It is not the philosophy that is important, it is the *doing*," and it is living in relationship with God that motivates what we choose to do.

AUTHORITY AND LEADERSHIP:

Torah is the final authority in Judaism. Because Judaism is a text-based religion (i.e., we have the Torah), for centuries the primary authorities in the religious community have been those who studied, taught and exemplified the values of the primary text. That would be Rabbis. As our world has changed, whole new categories of Jewish professional and volunteer authorities have evolved; educators, cantors, university professors, social workers, synagogue presidents and board members, and commu-

JEWISH WEDDING ON THE BEACH.

nal administrators are all part of the body of contemporary Jewish leadership. Still Torah remains the primary religious authority.

On the issue of *textual* authority, the modern Jewish world is very different than the ancient. Those who believe that God wrote and/or dictated the Torah to Moses still feel obligated to follow each and every one of the commandments in the text. The matter is very simple: "God said so." In communities that feel differently and describe the historical Torah as a part (although the most important part) of our dialogue with God's presence, there is a human component to the authorship of Jewish values and beliefs. People choose to observe commandments because they bring meaning and holiness to their lives; the obligation is often freely self-imposed.

CELEBRATIONS AND RITUALS: Like every religious civilization, Judaism has developed a long list of rituals. Many of them are associated with those moments in our personal life in which we observe significant change or growth. They are usually referred to as life-cycle events, and by now you've probably experienced a few of them within the life of your family. Implicit in many of them are some of the most significant values of Jewish teaching; for example, when you recently became a bar or bat mitzvah you were celebrating not simply your Jewish adult responsibility, but also important Jewish principles such as learning and teaching, assuming responsibility for the world in which you live and acknowledging the commanding presence of God.

Other celebrations, holidays, acknowledge important historical events in the history of our people and what they teach us about being a Jew. For example, perhaps the most important of these is Passover, which acknowledges the importance of freedom and our special obligation to remember the "heart of the stranger," for once upon a time we were strangers in the land of Egypt. Without Passover there are no Jews and there is no Judaism. Only two holidays, Rosh Ha-Shanah and Yom Kippur, have nothing to do with our people's history; but of course, they have everything to do with our personal history and how we live as Jewish people of faith.

◆ ◆ ◆ ◆

What might be a different definition for mitzvah other than commandment? How about "sacred opportunity" or "sacred obligation"? What do these terms imply?

SALVATION, OUR PLACE IN THE WORLD, THE BIG "MEANING OF LIFE" QUESTIONS: Though Jewish thought has some discussion of what philosophers call "salvation"—the ways in which we are "saved" from the inescapable reality of death—Judaism is primarily concerned with how we save the world from the cruelties of injustice. That is the primary lesson of Passover, our most formative experience, and it is what you have recognized every religious school morning when your teacher reminded you to contribute to *tzedakah*, the obligation to do what is right. It is not charity; it is justice.

In the Torah there are many stories told of God doing what is right. They are valued stories because they reflect the teaching of Genesis that human beings are created in the image of God, and we are therefore most human when we do what God would do.

IN OTHER WORDS—SOME CORE JEWISH VALUES:
When religions work through the four basic elements of religion as they see them, out come what we may call their "core values" and beliefs. We'll try to do that, in some way or other, for each of the religions we will study. In the meantime, I bet that every once in a while you'd like to have a nifty laminated card to keep in your pocket with the five basic things you need to know about Judaism to define its absolutely central teachings. So cut out the list on the following page and take it to your friendly laminator.

BRIT OLAM: Jews live in an everlasting covenant with God.

B'TZELEM ELOHIM: Human beings are created in the image of God; therefore we imitate Divine behavior and honor the image of God that is in every person.

TIKKUN OLAM: We are partners with God in the task of "repairing the world" because it just hasn't turned out the way it was supposed to.

TALMUD TORAH: The best Jew is a learned Jew; therefore the study of Torah (Jewish learning) is essential to authentic Jewish behavior.

AHAVAT YISRAEL: The love of the Jewish people is what makes our survival possible, and without our survival we wouldn't be able to do the other four things before this one. Included in our love for the Jewish people is our love for the land of our people, *Eretz Yisrael.* This concept also includes such things as the preservation and practice of what uniquely identifies us as Jews, such as the speaking of Hebrew.

Torah Study

It would be really hard to find the essence of Judaism in two short texts. But these two are a pretty good start. Read these texts. Answer the questions with a partner. Discuss them as a class.

Exodus 13.6–8: SEVEN DAYS YOU SHALL EAT UNLEAVENED BREAD, AND ON THE SEVENTH DAY THERE SHALL BE A FEAST TO THE ETERNAL. UNLEAVENED BREAD SHALL BE EATEN FOR SEVEN DAYS; NO LEAVENED BREAD SHALL BE SEEN WITH YOU, AND NO LEAVEN SHALL BE SEEN WITH YOU IN ALL YOUR TERRITORY. AND YOU SHALL TELL YOUR CHILD ON THAT DAY, "IT IS BECAUSE OF WHAT THE ETERNAL DID FOR ME WHEN I CAME OUT OF EGYPT."

1. What holiday is this passage discussing?
2. What three things does it ask you to do?
3. What is the connection between those three things?
4. What does matzah teach us?
5. In the Talmud it says "Every Jew is required to see him/herself as if s/he personally went out of Egypt." How is this learned from this passage? What is the importance of making the Exodus a personal experience rather than a historical memory?" (God took *me* out of Egypt, not God took *them* out of Egypt).
6. What is Jewish about this personal memory of the Exodus?
7. How do other Jewish holidays relive moments from Jewish history?

Deuteronomy 29.9: YOU STAND THIS DAY ALL OF YOU BEFORE THE ETERNAL, YOUR GOD; THE HEADS OF YOUR TRIBES, YOUR ELDERS, AND YOUR OFFICERS, ALL THE PEOPLE OF ISRAEL, YOUR LITTLE ONES, YOUR WIVES, AND THE RESIDENT-ALIENS WHO ARE IN YOUR CAMP, BOTH THE PERSON WHO CUTS YOUR WOOD AND THE PERSON WHO DRAWS YOUR WATER, THAT YOU MAY ENTER INTO THE SWORN COVENANT OF THE ETERNAL, YOUR GOD, WHICH THE ETERNAL, YOUR GOD, MAKES WITH YOU THIS DAY; THAT GOD MAY ESTABLISH YOU THIS DAY AS GOD'S PEOPLE, AND THAT GOD MAY BE YOUR GOD, AS WAS PROMISED TO YOU, AND AS GOD SWORE TO YOUR FATHERS, TO ABRAHAM, TO ISAAC, AND TO JACOB. NOT ONLY IS IT WITH YOU THAT I MAKE THIS SWORN COVENANT, BUT WITH THOSE WHO ARE NOT HERE WITH US THIS DAY AS WELL AS WITH THOSE WHO STAND HERE WITH US THIS DAY BEFORE THE ETERNAL OUR GOD.

8. The center of this text is the making of a covenant. What is a covenant? What is the covenant between God and Israel?
9. Who does this text include in the covenant?

10. What does it mean when it says "Not only is it with you that I make this sworn covenant, but with those who are not here with us this day as well"?

11. This text is one of those that establish the idea of the "Chosen People." What does that concept mean to you?

Here is a famous Hasidic story.

The Holy Maggid of Mezrich was an important, world-class Hasidic teacher. He took over from the son of the Baal Shem Tov and became the Rebbe of all Hasidic Jews. But before he was discovered and became a great rebbe, he earned his living as a ordinary Hebrew school teacher in a heder. Later, after he became famous, people became interested in his past. They went to his Hebrew school students and asked them, "What kind of teacher was he?"

One student answered: "He pushed us and pulled us. He asked us questions and he listened to us. He waited until each one of us told him his own story of what it was like to go out of Egypt and cross the Reed Sea. And he waited until each one of us told him his own story of what it was like to stand at Mt. Sinai and accept the Torah."

(Retold from Martin Buber, *Tales of the Hasidim*)

12. How is this story connected to these two Torah texts? What does it tell us about being a Jew?

PRAYERS CRAMMED INTO THE WESTERN WALL

30

Basic Judaism

To conclude, use this chapter and fill in the following categories:

1. **GOD AND FAITH** (Who is the God, and what are you supposed to believe?)

   _____

   _____

   _____

2. **AUTHORITY AND LEADERSHIP** (Who are the leaders of Judaism, and what authority do they have?)

   _____

   _____

   _____

3. **REVELATION** (How does God communicate with people?)

   _____

   _____

   _____

4. **CELEBRATION** (What are the major holidays, and how are they celebrated?)

   _____

   _____

   _____

5. **SALVATION** (What is "saved," and how do you get there?)

   _____

   _____

   _____

6. **THE MEANING OF LIFE** (What is the purpose of living?)

_____

_____

_____

7. **CORE VALUES** (What are this religion's most important values?)

_____

_____

_____

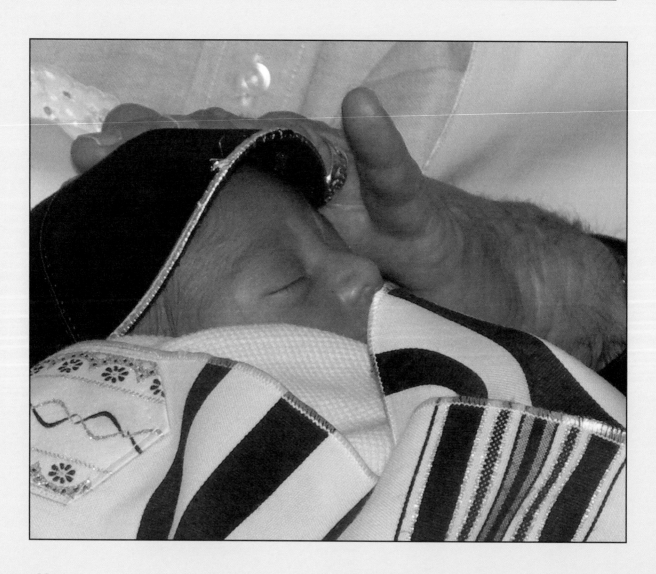

Chapter 3.
A Really, Really Brief History of Christianity

Basic Jesus

You've probably never studied the life of Jesus. But you've also probably learned a lot about him from TV, movies, and other media. Work with a partner and see if you can put the life of Jesus in order.

_____ After Jesus' birth, the couple was forced to use a manger in place of a crib because there was no room for them at the inn.

_____ Jesus died on the cross at Calvary, which was also called Golgotha. His body was placed in a tomb.

_____ Jesus came to the Jordan River where John the Baptist had been baptizing people. He baptized Jesus.

_____ Jesus was turned him over to the Roman leader Pontius Pilate based on an accusation of claiming to be King of the Jews.

_____ Jesus was born in Bethlehem to Mary, a virgin. Mary and Joseph were forced to leave their homes in Nazareth and come to the home of Joseph's ancestors for a census.

_____ Jesus attracted crowds numbering in the thousands and delivered the Sermon on the Mount.

_____ Jesus came with his followers to Jerusalem during the Passover festival, and a large crowd came to meet him.

_____ Jesus rose from the dead on the third day after his crucifixion.

_____ An angel announced Jesus' birth to shepherds who came to see the newborn child. Magi also brought gifts to the infant after following a star they believed was a sign.

_____ Jesus celebrated a final meal with his disciples. This became known as the Last Supper.

_____ Jesus created a disturbance at the Temple by overturning the tables of the moneylenders who set up shop there.

_____ Jesus performed miracles including healings, walking on water, turning water into wine, and raising Lazarus from the dead.

This is the order in which the four gospels appear in the Christian Scriptures: Matthew, Mark, Luke and John. Most scholars agree, however, that Mark is probably the earliest of the four, perhaps written down somewhere around 70 C.E. The original Greek texts of the four gospels have been gone for a very long time.

Christian Beginnings

The story of Christianity begins with the life story of Jesus as recorded in the **NEW TESTAMENT**. Christians call it the "New" Testament, because they believe it is a successor to the Hebrew Bible, which Christians call the "Old" Testament. Most scholars (and Jews) refer to the books of the "New Testament" as the Christian Scriptures. There are four different versions of the life of Jesus as recorded in the four **SYNOPTIC GOSPELS**, Matthew, Mark, Luke and John.

Though the story is pretty much the same, each of them is slightly different and emphasizes various aspects of Jesus' life and teachings that are of importance to the author. Within a hundred years or so after the death of Jesus, the Christian Scriptures was completed with the addition of letters written by Paul, an early follower of Jesus, and various others. Paul wrote these letters to different communities in order to explain the stories and teachings of Jesus and the basic ideas of the new Christian church, and for all practical purposes it was Paul who created what we know as the origins of the religion of Christianity.

MARY FROM THE CATHEDRAL OF ST. JOHN IN SAVANNAH, GEORGIA.
© ROBERT YOUNG

The life story of Jesus, some of which may be familiar to you, takes place, more or less, over the first third of the first century of the Common Era. While there are some who argue that an historical person named Jesus may never have existed, mainstream scholarship and popular belief assume or believe that he did. No serious Jewish literature doubts the existence of Jesus either. People do argue, of course, about what his life and teachings mean, but it makes little sense at this point to doubt that he did exist. The Christian Scriptures tells us that Jesus was born to his parents, Mary and Joseph, "by the Holy Spirit," meaning that Mary was still a virgin. This idea is called the

CHRIST THE REDEEMER ON CORCOVADO MOUNTAIN, RIO DE JANEIRO BRAZIL SOUTH AMERICA THE STATUE STANDS 125 FEET TALL AND IS LOCATED AT THE PEAK OF THE CORCOVADO MOUNTAIN.

© DAVID DAVIS

IMMACULATE CONCEPTION and has much to do with the spiritual (i.e., not physical) idea that Jesus is the Son of God, in a definition of God known as the **TRINITY**.

Jesus grew up in the city of Nazareth in Northern Israel. (He may even have become a bar mitzvah, though probably not in the same way as you.)

We learn from various stories that as he grew he was well known for his devotion to learning and for the eloquence of his teaching. A popular traveling preacher named John the Baptist (or **BAPTIZER**) predicted that the world was about to change and it was time for Jewish people to repent of their past sins. Something about Jesus caught John's attention, and he baptized him, immersing him in the waters of the Jordan River. Because John was so popular, this gave Jesus a certain power and credibility throughout the land. Shortly after his baptism Jesus resisted a temptation by the devil (Matthew 4:1–11), and his fame began to grow. He began to gather a group of **DISCIPLES.**

In the Gospel of Luke (2:41-51) a story is told that could be interpreted as a bar mitzvah-like event, in terms of what we know about ritual life in the days of the Temple in Jerusalem. Jesus was actually twelve at the time of this story, and the story is told to demonstrate what a smart kid he was.

The Sermon on the Mount including the so-called "Beatitudes", along with the many stories and parables of the New Testament, brings up the question of how religion is taught and whether Jesus was following in the traditions and styles of our Rabbis. In fact, he is often referred to as Rabbi. In a small example, Matthew reports that Jesus gave a long sermon (that's how you know for sure he wanted to be a rabbi—it's long) sitting down. The Rabbis of that time always taught sitting down, even though paintings of this immense event always show Jesus standing on the hillside next to the Sea of Galilee with thousands of people gathered around. Why are parables and metaphors and similes so often used? What exactly is a *midrash*? Why is religion so difficult to teach and, conversely, so difficult to understand? Our Rabbis used all of these techniques; they still do.

IMAGE OF A CEMETERY STATUE OF THE CRUCIFIXION OF JESUS CHRIST.   © PHOTOS BY RYASICK

For many years Jesus went throughout the land of Israel teaching and telling stories. Some of these sermons and stories were very popular, including, for example, the Sermon on the Mount (Matthew 5:1-7:27). The Christian Scriptures also records many miracles that he performed, such as healing the sick and finding food for the hungry when there was none to be had. Many of his teachings were critical of the Judaism of his time, though he never advocated the creation of a different religion, and he urged the Jews to follow the *mitzvot* of the Torah.

In time, the story is told, the Roman government of Israel began to worry about the popularity of Jesus. The Christian Scriptures records that so did some of the Jewish leadership. The story of his last supper with his disciples, his arrest by the Roman authorities, the supposed involvement of the Jewish leadership and his execution by **CRUCIFIXION** is one of the most famous, complicated and passionate stories of all time. (That's why it's often referred to as "The Passion"). But the most important part of the story is what Christianity refers to as the **RESURRECTION**, when three days after Jesus died on the cross he apparently came back to life and met again with his disciples. In all of these stories you will find the birth of the most significant concepts of the Christian faith; and in the differing interpretations of these stories you will find many of the origins of the different branches of Christianity.

◆ ◆ ◆ ◆

Over the next century, during the height of the Roman Empire, Christianity began to spread through what is known as the Mediterranean basin. Many Christian communities were established. As the disciples turned to other countries, the authors of the Christian Scriptures helped to clarify what the story of Jesus taught. Paul, in particular, added brand-new ideas, rituals and concepts that were never a part of Judaism. Some of these are the ideas of **ORIGINAL SIN, THE SECOND COMING** and the belief that human beings cannot achieve **SALVATION** through their own actions, only through their faith in Jesus. Later on there were also different views on the power of **FAITH** and **WORKS** that were critical in the divisions that took place. But in any case, the life story of Jesus, especially the Resurrection, and the further teachings of the Christian Scriptures lead to the core value of Christian belief that **JESUS IS MESSIAH, THE CHRIST**, and that he will save the world from sin and death.

In the fourth century of the Common Era Christianity had become so popular that it became the official religion of the Roman Empire and was centered in Rome. This was the birth of the Catholic Church, to this day the largest expression of Christianity in the world. It was also the beginning of the leadership of the Church by the Popes.

But over the centuries there were many variations and new ideas about the teachings of Jesus and his disciples. Some of these arguments were quite bitter; many, in fact, led to either wars of words or real wars with all horrible results. Many of the wars happened because different countries assumed one of the variations of Christianity as their national religion and wished to spread their beliefs to others.

The largest break-offs from the Catholic Church included the Eastern, Greek and Russian Orthodox communities and, of course, the many different **PROTESTANT** (think "protest") churches. Most of the "protesting" began in Western Europe at the transition from medieval to early modern times, the most famous being that begun by Martin Luther (1483-1546 C.E.). In time, all or most of them came to America, and you know

It is a common Christian tradition that Jesus "ordained" his disciple Peter (originally named Simon) as the first Pope. It is also the first Christian pun (a play on words)! In Matthew 16:13-20 Simon-Peter affirms that Jesus is "the Christ, the Son of the Living God." Jesus responds that Peter could only have known this because God told him so, and he therefore says to Peter, "You are Peter, and on this rock I will build my church" (16:18). In Greek, Peter is *petros* and rock is *petra* (the same similarity occurs in Latin, only it's a different word). This means that Jesus sees Peter as the foundation of his church, and of course, the big church in Rome where the Pope works is St. Peter's, and he sits in St. Peter's Chair. There is even a tomb deep under the Vatican that is said to be the burial place of Peter.

SAINT PETER'S DOME (BASILICA DI SAN PIETRO) FROM TEVERE RIVER, VATICAN TOWN, ROME, ITALY. © ROCA

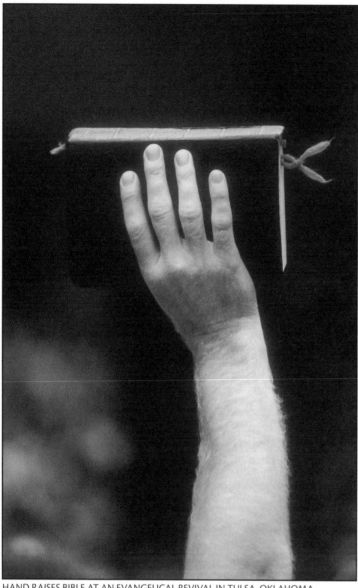

HAND RAISES BIBLE AT AN EVANGELICAL REVIVAL IN TULSA, OKLAHOMA
© ANNIE GRIFFITHS BELT/CORBIS

them by such names as Lutheran, Methodist, Presbyterian, Baptist, and many other different kinds of Protestants. But not all of them broke off from Catholicism; many of them broke off from each other, including some that are still doing so today, such as the large **EVANGELICAL** communities in the United States.

Because Christianity is so diverse, it will be difficult to compare Judaism to each of the many different Christian denominations. Instead we will examine the relationship between basic Jewish teachings and some of the ideas and beliefs highlighted in this history. These ideas are still relevant to all forms of Christianity, though there will be some different ways in which they are emphasized and in which ideas are really important to the particular denomination. And in particular, one of the important ideas we have to think about is a difficult Christian concept (difficult for us especially) that the Church (the Christian community) is the **NEW ISRAEL** and that Christians have established a **NEW COVENANT** with God replacing that of the Jewish people. It is this idea that in great part has moved many Christians to become **PROSELYTIZERS** and try to convert Jews to Christianity and to accept Jesus as Messiah. You are probably familiar with this reality, and after we finish our comparison between Judaism and Christianity we'll pay some attention to this issue, too.

Mormons

Many people are not certain if the Mormons are Christians, and since you probably run across them from time to time, it is certainly worth our while to spend a few moments familiarizing ourselves with this very active and involved religious community.

The Mormons are definitely Christians, though there are some Christian critics who say that they're not. Their full name is The Church of Latter Day Saints of Jesus Christ, and they accept and, in their own way, practice all of the doctrines of classical Christian belief. What they mean by "latter day saints" (LDS is a name by which they also call themselves) is that their primary prophet, Joseph Smith, received a call from God in the 1820s (hence the "latter days") to revive the original teachings of the Christians of the early days. This included many kinds of Christian doctrines and practices that were mentioned in the Christian Scriptures and other places (The Book of Mormon) but were not necessarily practiced any longer, as well as all of the other basic beliefs of Christianity. It was Joseph Smith who formed this group of latter day saints, and it was his immedi-

MORMON TEMPLE, SALT LAKE CITY UTAH .   © BEN C.

ate followers who brought the Church to Utah to escape from angry attacks in the more settled parts of the United States. Today the worldwide headquarters of the Mormon Church is in Salt Lake City, and there are some twelve million members around the globe.

Much of their doctrine comes from The Book of Mormon. The Book of Mormon is belived to be based on records kept by prophets who were descendants of the ancient House of Israel (that would be us) who lived in the New World, in Central America, between 600 B.C.E. and 400 C.E. The book contains a record of God's relationship with them and the story of how Jesus came and ministered to them in the New World after his resurrection. The ancient records were abridged and edited by the prophet Moroni and engraved on gold plates in order to preserve them. Joseph Smith was "commissioned" by God to translate the book, and the Church began in 19th century.

There is much more to know about the LDS. They have a unique organizational structure; they have serious commitments to family life and to health concerns about eating and drinking. They do much proselytizing, and most of their young people serve two years as missionaries in countries around the world. Some people think they are secretive and separatist, and many people do not really understand who and what they believe, despite their prominence in many American communities. Many Jewish people are upset about a particular Mormon practice of "baptizing in absentia" Jewish people after they died, and the Mormon church has promised to end this practice. But while I hope you will learn more about them, should you wish, for now, since they are Christians and believe in major Christian doctrine, we will include them in our comparisons of Judaism and Christianity.

In summary, I'll rephrase the **CORE VALUES and BELIEFS** of Christianity, just as we did with Judaism. I don't know if you'll want to laminate these and keep them in your pocket, because who knows what your Mom will say when she finds them in the laundry? Nonetheless, it's a good idea to know these before we go ahead and compare Christianity and Judaism. These are the ideas that are central to just about all Christian denominations:

VAN COVERED WITH RELIGIOUS
GRAFFITI
© LORI SKELTON

1. Jesus is the Messiah (Savior), and by believing in him and the miracles of his life story, such as the Immaculate Conception, individual Christians can find Salvation and everlasting life.

2. People who are not "saved" will experience everlasting death. Since being saved requires having faith in Jesus, people who do not accept Jesus as Lord and Savior are not able to be forgiven for their human sins, and they are punished. This punishment is called Hell.

3. Jesus died on the cross and was resurrected as a proof that belief in him can save one from death.

4. Humankind is born with an "original sin" because of Adam, and it is part of our human identity. Faith in Jesus (and in many cases, through the doing of good works) can ease and/ or remove this burden.

5. The arrival of Christianity in the world meant the rewriting of the Covenant between God and Israel. Christianity is the new Israel, and only Christians can achieve true salvation. (However, this concept is modified and/or ignored in many modern and liberal Christian faiths out of respect for Jews and Judaism.)

6. Jesus will return to bring the ultimate salvation of humankind.

7. God has three aspects: the Father, the Son and the Holy Spirit. This concept of the Trinity makes it possible for Christians to believe that God, as Jesus, appeared on the earth.

A Basic Vocabulary of Christianity

NEW TESTAMENT: The basic text of Christianity, the Christian Scriptures is an anthology of several different kinds of literary styles about the life and teachings of Jesus and the early Christian community. A testament is, obviously, a testimony about something you know or have experienced. The many books of the Christian Scriptures were assembled in the first hundred years after the death of Jesus. Four of them are referred to as the **SYNOPTIC GOSPELS**; "synoptic" usually means the sharing of a similar view, and "gospel" is from an old Anglo-Saxon term meaning "good tidings". These books tell the life story of Jesus. Most of the remaining books of the Christian Scriptures are letters by Paul or other leaders of early Christianity, and the last book of the Christian Scriptures, Revelation, is particularly interesting. It is what is referred to as "apocalyptic," an end-of-the-world sort of thing in which God's plan for the future is revealed.

A PRIEST GIVING THE HOLY SACRAMENT
© VIM WOODENHANDS

It is interesting to note that in Hebrew the Christian Scriptures is referred to as **THE NEW COVENANT** ברית חדשה, because early Christians believed that Christianity would replace Judaism as the expression of the covenant, the relationship between God and the Jewish people. (Yes, there are translations of the Christian Scriptures into Hebrew; can you guess why?)

APOSTLE: Normally a term for people sent on a mission, the word "apostle" has come to mean specifically the twelve apostles of Jesus who were also referred to as his **disciples**, and Paul. Paul was the most active missionary on behalf of the early Church, and he is held in a higher regard than the twelve apostles. The height of his career seems to be between 54 and 58 of the Common Era.

Jesus had twelve disciples, or students, who were his constant companions and who also spread the messages that he was teaching. Their names were Simon (later renamed Peter), Andrew, James, John, Philip, Bartholomew, Thomas, Matthew, James, Thaddeus, Simon and Judas. You might like to read the tenth chapter of Matthew, in which Jesus consecrates or commissions his disciples and gives them their job description.

IMMACULATE CONCEPTION: One of the most difficult concepts for non-Christians to appreciate, the notion of the so-called "virgin birth" is not as much about Mary as it is about Jesus. For Christians, Jesus is both divine and human, and that means that he cannot have been born in the same way as the rest of us. In fact, according to Christianity, he wasn't so much born as he was sent. To humans, his birth is a miracle and makes him worthy of human attention.

A COUPLE PRAYS TOGETHER AT A TABLE AS THEIR HANDS REST UPON THEIR HOLY BIBLES.

© LINCOLN ROGERS

You may have seen that guy who always seems to be sitting in the end zone at football games holding a sign that says, "John 3:16". He usually has a funny colored wig. He is most likely a zealous Christian missionary urging the TV football audience to read from the Gospel according to John. The verse says "For God so loved the world that He gave His only son, that whoever believes in him (the son) shall not perish, but have eternal life." When you read this verse that Martin Luther (his name will come up again soon) called the "gospel in miniature," you are encountering the core teaching of this story and one of the core beliefs of Christianity: Jesus' arrival in the world is a miraculous moment in human history and is intended by "God the Father" to give humankind new hope.

TRINITY: Another "most difficult concept" is about the notion that God has three aspects but is still One. The three parts are God, the Son and the Holy Spirit (often referred to as the Holy Ghost). The Christian God can become flesh; that would be Jesus. The connective force between the two is the Holy Spirit. This idea is important in understanding some of the teachings of the Christian Scriptures and is accepted with only minor variations in contemporary Christian communities.

BAPTIZER: It's difficult to know when John baptized Jesus, (you can read the story in Chapter 3 of the book of Matthew) if he was imitating or expanding the Jewish concept of the ritual bath (the *mikveh*), or if he was creating some new idea. Baptism (immersion in water) has become an important part of Christian ritual, although there still remain significant differences of opinion on how it is to be done. These differences range from complete immersion to sprinkling. There are also different interpretations of what it may mean in the life of a Christian person. Sometimes it is about conversion to Christianity; some people think of it as something only for newborn children; and some adults will undertake the ritual quite often. But it is clearly not about the idea of ritual purification or cleansing, which is the common understanding of the Jewish ritual bath. Baptism is an imitation of a critical part of the life story of Jesus, his death and resurrection. Going under the water is symbolic death; coming out of it is returning to life. The faith that the "baptizee" expresses by allowing himself or herself to go into the water symbolizes a faith in the redeeming power of Jesus and an expression of the belief that life can and will go on after death. It is one of the ways to demonstrate that you are a "Christ"-ian, a person who believes in what Jesus taught in the experiences of his life.

CRUCIFIXION: The custom of executing common criminals by nailing them to a crucifix, (a crude cross of wood) was the standard Roman form of capital punishment. It was terribly painful, and the victim did not usually die immediately, which allowed time for some final words. According to many Christian thinkers, Jesus felt that it was necessary for him to die; otherwise he would not be able to return and prove his divinity. Therefore, in his view, the Romans were but instruments in the story. Nonetheless, in his pain the Christian Scriptures records that Jesus, paraphrasing from Psalm 22, says, "My God, my God, why have You forsaken me?"

RESURRECTION: As we've discussed already, three days after he was executed on the cross, Jesus miraculously reappeared among his disciples and spent time with them, reminding them of their responsibilities. In time the celebration of the Resurrection became the most important expression of Christian faith; you know it as Easter, and it is the central holy day of Christian life. Without the miracle of the Resurrection there is no Christianity. It embodies the central teaching of Christianity that faith in the life story and teachings of Jesus delivers (or "saves") the Christian from everlasting death and the sinfulness of human life.

ORIGINAL SIN: Christianity teaches that because of the failure, or fall, of Adam in the Garden of Eden stories, all human beings are born into sin. Adam is the model or paradigm of what it means to be a human, and therefore, by our very nature as descendents of the first human, we are sinners, and we are incapable of escaping from our nature by ourselves. It's just who we are. But baptism and faith in Jesus free us from that original sinfulness, and we can be forgiven. Hence all the signs you may see (and make bad jokes about) that "Jesus Saves". It is a very serious matter at the center of Christian belief; Jesus is the only way you can be saved (achieve salvation) from both the sinful nature of being a human and from the punishment (Hell) that sinners receive and saved people do not.

THE SECOND COMING: It is not clear when this idea became part of Christian thought, but it is certainly related to the realization that none of the predictions made in the Christian Scriptures have ever happened. The idea of the Second Coming was developed to say that the fullness of Jesus' Messianic predictions would happen only when he returned for a second time. Since the development of this idea, all kinds of suggestions have been made as to what would indicate to the world that the Second Coming was occurring; some of those suggestions involve Jews and Judaism.

SALVATION: We've already studied a little about the idea of Salvation. It is a concept that in one way or another is important to most religions and has to do, as the word implies, with being saved from something—death or meaninglessness or sin or injustice. Believers in Jesus are saved from both sin and everlasting death. Christianity has a very clear concept of a life after death that seems to imply that you don't die; you just move on to a different level of life. Your faith in Jesus frees you from the original sin of human nature, and that makes it possible for you to find everlasting life.

FAITH AND WORKS: In religious expressions that seek salvation there are generally two different ways to achieve it: having absolute faith in the teachings of your religious leader or system, or working really hard to achieve it by yourself through the things that you do. As we have seen, Christianity strongly emphasizes that only faith in Jesus can bring salvation, because human beings suffer from the problem of original sin. As we will study later, Judaism emphasizes the things that you *do*, usually defined as the *mitzvot* or commandments of Jewish religious law and teaching. However, this important difference is a matter of emphasis, because each religion does have some of the other within it. The really interesting thing is that Jesus urged his followers to observe the commandments and Jewish law; it was only after his death and the destruction of the Temple in Jerusalem that Christianity introduced the new concept of salvation through faith.

WOMAN IN AN OUTDOORS SETTING PRAISING AND WORSHIPING

© RUSSELL SHIVELY

JESUS IS MESSIAH: The word "messiah" as a religious concept is most easily understood to mean the person, being, or process that

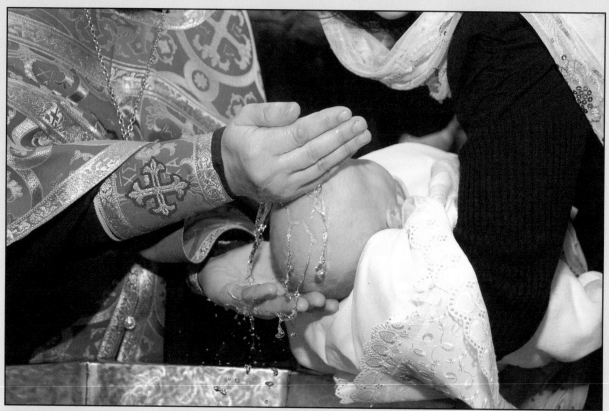

brings salvation, whatever it is that salvation means for that particular religious system. The English word "Messiah" comes originally from the Hebrew *mashiah*, which means "the anointed one". (Anointing is usually done by pouring oil on the head of the person to be anointed.) In the *Tanakh* (the Hebrew Bible) King David is anointed as the leader (political, military and social sovereign) of Israel by the prophet and judge Samuel. (It is interesting to note that many medieval Christian artists painted Jesus as looking like the Biblical description of King David, someone with reddish hair and a ruddy complexion.) In Christianity Jesus is anointed by John the Baptist. "Christ" is a Greek word for "anointed" as well, and it used to be that people said Jesus the Christ, the anointed. People who are Christians believe that Jesus is the Messiah, the Christ. And in some interpretations the word has to do with naming as, for example, when a ship is *christened* with a ceremony that actually looks a little bit like a baptism. Christian children are often named at the time of their baptism.

PROTESTANT: In 1529 a group of German princes and cities supported the protest of Martin Luther against certain teachings of Catholicism. These particular teachings were about the authority of the Pope, a difference of opinion on faith alone, the Bible as the only source of truth, and a few other important issues. In time this protest by Luther gave rise to the Lutheran Church and other Christian religious expressions, all gathered under the name of Protest-ants, people who protested against basic Catholic teachings.

EVANGELICAL: The Latin origin of this word is related to the word "gospel," which, as we saw before, means good news. For the most part, it defines a conservative or fundamentalist kind of Christianity that emphasizes the primacy of the Christian Scriptures over the other teachings or interpretations of Christianity that have been developed since then. Evangelicals can be understood as people who seek fervently to help others commit to a faith in Jesus, to accept Jesus as their savior. People who are evangelicals are therefore very involved with preaching, proselytizing and converting non-Christians to Christianity.

PROSELYTIZING: People who proselytize are people who try to convert others, or change the minds of others, about ideas or beliefs. In the religious world proselytizers are often called "missionaries," and they try to convert people of other faiths to their religion. As with many of our vocabulary words, this one also has Greek origins and has to do with bringing someone "near."

Exercise

Here is John 3.16-19, one of the more basic texts on how and why it was that Jesus showed up.

> For God so loved the world that God gave his only Son, that whoever believes in Him should not perish but have eternal life. For God sent the Son into the world, not to condemn the world, but that the world might be saved through Him. People who believe in Him are not condemned; people who do not believe are condemned already, because they have not believed in the name of the only Son of God. And this is the judgment, that the light has come into the world, and people loved darkness rather than light, because their deeds were evil.

A WOMAN IS PRAYING TO GOD WITH HOPE

© MEHMET ALCI

1. What is the "big idea" of this passage? _____

_____

2. According to it, what does it take to be saved? _____

_____

3. What do you think "saved" means? _____

_____

4. What does John mean when he says "And people loved darkness rather than light, because their deeds were evil"? _____

_____

5. Is this idea that God sends a child to save the world a Jewish idea?_____

_____

Basic Christianity

To conclude, use this chapter and fill in the following categories.

1. **GOD AND FAITH** (Who is the God, and what are you supposed to believe?)

   _____

   _____

   _____

2. **AUTHORITY AND LEADERSHIP** (Who are the leaders of Christianity, and what authority do they have? Be careful; different denominations have different kinds of leadership).

   _____

   _____

   _____

3. **REVELATION** (How does God communicate with people?)

   _____

   _____

   _____

4. **CELEBRATION** (What are the major holidays, and how are they celebrated?)

   _____

   _____

   _____

5. **SALVATION** (What is "saved," and how do you get there?)

   _____

   _____

   _____

6. **THE MEANING OF LIFE** (What is the purpose of living?)

_____

_____

_____

7. **CORE VALUES** (What are this religion's most important values?)

_____

_____

_____

PROCESSION OF HOLY SACRAMENT
© JOZEF SEDMAK

Chapter 4.
Comparing Judaism and Christianity

The Nicene Creed

The purpose of a creed is to act as a yardstick of correct belief. A creed is a focus, not a full definition, of what is required for orthodoxy. It was hoped that by memorizing this summary of the faith, lay people without extensive theological training would be able to recognize deviations from orthodox doctrines based on the Bible as interpreted in Christian tradition.

The original Nicene Creed was first adopted in 325 at the First Council of Nicaea. At that time the text ended after the words "We believe in the Holy Spirit." It is the central tenet of Catholic belief. Read it with a partner. Underline the parts that you feel you can accept as a Jew.

We believe in one God,
the Father, the Almighty,
maker of heaven and earth,
of all that is, seen and unseen.
We believe in one Lord, Jesus Christ,
the only Son of God,
eternally begotten of the Father,
God from God, Light from Light,
true God from true God,
begotten, not made,
of one Being with the Father;
through him all things were made.
For us and for our salvation
he came down from heaven,
was incarnate of the Holy Spirit and the Virgin Mary
and became truly human.
For our sake he was crucified under Pontius Pilate;
he suffered death and was buried.
On the third day he rose again
in accordance with the Scriptures;
he ascended into heaven
and is seated at the right hand of the Father.
He will come again in glory to judge the living and the dead,
and his kingdom will have no end.
We believe in the Holy Spirit, the Lord, the giver of life,
who proceeds from the Father and the Son,
who with the Father and the Son is worshiped and glorified,
who has spoken through the prophets.
We believe in one holy catholic and apostolic Church.
We acknowledge one baptism for the forgiveness of sins.
We look for the resurrection of the dead,
and the life of the world to come. Amen. (1988 ecumenical version)

List ten things that Judaism and Christianity share as beliefs.

1._____

_____

2._____

_____

3._____

_____

4._____

_____

5._____

_____

6._____

_____

7._____

_____

8._____

_____

9._____

_____

10._____

_____

The Comparison

Whenever you approach the comparison of Judaism and Christianity, you will almost always hear a well-intentioned mention of our shared Judeo-Christian heritage. This is especially true in the United States, but also so in most of Western civilization. The notion that we have shared values is most likely born in the recognition that Christianity grew from Jewish roots. The Jewish Bible is sacred text to the Christians; its teachings are part of Christian belief; it is the accepted word of God.

The roots of Christianity, like those of a tree, are in the world of Jewish life and teachings in which Jesus and the disciples lived. But before too long some branches of the tree bore the fruit of Christian ideas and beliefs. Still, we do share some important DNA.

The reality, however, is much more complicated than that, and the truth of the matter is that within the factors that define "religious expression" Judaism and Christianity are very different religious expressions in many ways. America does have a rich tradition of Jews and Christians sharing common goals and hopes for our society, the so-called Judeo-Christian heritage, but that does not mean that our *religions* are alike. In fact, they are not. When it comes to the categories that define a religion, as we learned in our first lesson, Judaism and Christianity are not just oranges and apples, they are lions and butterflies. (I'm only speaking about lions and butterflies to make a symbolic point here; don't get all excited trying to figure out which one is which.)

To show that this is so, or mostly so, we'll return to the categories we discussed in our first lesson—the categories that, in general, help us define the central identifying factors of most religious expressions. *But first* a cautionary note about the comparisons that will follow.

One of the really interesting examples of this shared acceptance of our *Tanakh* is the use of biblical texts in the liturgy. Both Jewish and Christian worship, for instance, make a big deal out of Isaiah 6:2,

"קָדוֹשׁ
קָדוֹשׁ
קָדוֹשׁ

Holy, Holy Holy is the Lord of Hosts, the whole earth is full of God's glory."
It shouldn't be too hard to figure out why that sentence means so much to both faiths.

NEXT SUNDAY'S SERVICE
10 am

© GARY JAMES CALDER

There are more than two billion Christians in the world and about twelve million Jews. Those two billion Christians are divided into a huge number of religious denominations that are distinguished by significant differences of doctrine, practice and institutional structures. Judaism is divided, too, but we also share a common ethnic history in a way that, for the most part, Christians do not. We are a people as well as a religion, and that common history unites us in ways that make it a little easier to talk about shared beliefs for us than for Christians. That makes comparison between Judaism as a whole and Christianity as a whole very, very difficult. To do an absolutely thorough job we'd have to compare each part of Judaism with each part of Christianity. That's more complicated than Sudoku! So what follows is based on our ability to talk about common threads in all of Christianity compared with common threads in all of Judaism.

Sometimes it may appear that Christians have ethnic affiliations; Christmas looks very different in different Christian countries and communities. One could argue that Jewish ethnicity is different *in degree*, but you should begin to develop the idea that how we eat and talk is an act of Jewish identification as much as is our religious belief. That is very different from Christian behavior.

THE CREATION OF ADAM
BY MICHELANGELO
© THE GALLERY
COLLECTION/CORBIS

About God

Beliefs about God and our relationship with God constitute the first category we identified as an element in religious expression. You may remember that in our first lesson we learned that the Jewish ideas of God appear to emphasize our relationship with God more than what exactly God is. In fact, many Jewish texts teach that God is *Elohim Nistarim*, the "hidden God". No matter what we think we know, it is virtually impossible to know for sure the exact nature of the Divine Presence. The Bible's repeated assertion that humans "cannot see the face of God and live" is usually interpreted to mean that we are not *meant* to know the reality of God; we are only meant to live in a covenant with God. In all of our stories, only Moses is ever allowed to see the face of God (see Deuteronomy 34:10).

You could even say this about Judaism and God: If God becomes familiar (no longer a mystery), then God does not have the power and the authority to be the God that commands the things we are meant to do.

On the other hand, the principal story that defines Christianity is about that moment in time when God, as Jesus, appeared on earth "in the flesh" and thus declared a new reality about the nature of God. The core of Christianity is the belief that Jesus is the Messiah, that Jesus is the son of God, and that he walked on earth. He is both human and divine. You cannot be a Christian if you do not believe in that story, if you do not believe that God can become a physical being and walk among us. And you cannot be a Jew if you do.

The common definition of God in all streams of Christian thought is expressed through what is known as the Trinity. God has three aspects, one of which is the physical Jesus; the other two are the Father and the Holy Spirit. To a certain extent, it is possible to say that the Father retains some of the Jewish idea of the mystery and hidden-ness of God. God sends to earth the aspect of Himself that we can know and touch and feel, while His essence as the Father remains beyond our intellectual and physical reach.

Many scholars agree that this concept of divisibility comes from the intellectual traditions of the Greek and Roman world, but it really doesn't matter to us where it came from; it is the foundational Christian idea about God. God is one being with three distinct parts. Christians will tell you that Christianity is a monotheistic religion (a belief in one God), and it is. But it is important to remember that the Christian God is divisible into divine and flesh.

The Jewish God is neither divisible nor physical, although we sometimes talk as though God is. All religions have a problem with trying to find the right vocabulary to talk about God,

---

Some verses in the Bible are anthropomorphic; i.e., in them God does the kind of things that humans normally do. But you might wonder if the God of Mystery above the World of Worlds can be portrayed with essentially human attributes and in language we normally reserve for human actions.

"Come let us **descend** and there confound their language." (Gen. 11:7)

"And God **ascended** from Abraham." (Gen.17:22)

"What is man that You should **think** of him, and the son of man that You should visit him?" (Psalm 8:5)

"O God who **sits** in the heavens." (Psalm 123:1)

"Behold I will **stand** before you there upon the rock in Horeb." (Exodus 17:6)

"And I will **cover** you with My hand until I have **passed** before you." (Exodus 33:22)

"And I will **hide** My face from them. (Deut. 31:17)

And all of the hundreds of places where it says,

"And God spoke."

These words seem to give God a certain physical nature, but they are simply metaphors for the mysterious and mystical processes by which we discover and sense God in our lives.

because once you begin to say that God communicates with us, you have to use words like "talk," "appear," "command," "was really angry with us" and so on.

The great Jewish philosophers of the Middle Ages, like Maimonides, spent their entire careers trying to find other ways and other words to get around this problem. In fact, Maimonides gave us some interesting vocabulary to use in our comparison with Christianity. He taught us that not only is God One (and not three), but that "one" means something more than our belief that there is only God. "One" also means that God is perfect unity; God cannot be divided up into parts. This can be a very difficult piece of philosophy to talk about, and not all Jewish teachers agree with some of the consequences of Maimonides' philosophy, but for the moment, for us, it is a pretty clear statement of how Judaism and Christianity are different. One God means an indivisible God.

Finally, before we conclude our comparisons between Judaism and Christianity about God, we should spend a moment on an aspect of our thinking about God that is very popular these days: mysticism and spirituality.

Think Madonna and Kaballah

All religions share an element of mysticism, which in a few words is "the search for a direct, personal experience of God." The task of mystical teachers in all religions is to discuss their own experience and how they think others might achieve that same experience. Spirituality, in our time, is about the ways we think God's presence is found within us and made real in the way we live. People will say, "She is a very spiritual person," although sometimes it doesn't sound as if they are talking about Godliness, but about gentleness and calm and kindness. There are great mystical and spiritual teachers in both Judaism and Christianity; to experience God directly is something many deeply religious people seek. But as you could probably guess, the God that mystics seek is different in our two great faiths.

About Authority and Leadership

Once we finish our discussion about God, the issues of authority that remain for our comparison are about primary texts and about structural and institutional issues. Judaism considers Torah our primary text (and, to a lesser extent the rest of the Bible and later Rabbinic books) and does not consider the Christian Scriptures an authoritative text for us. Christianity, on the other hand, assumes the authority of our entire Bible, especially the Torah and the prophetic books, *and* the Christian Scriptures. Every Christian Bible contains both testaments. This happened because Christianity began as a part of Judaism, and in order to validate Jesus as the Messiah it was imperative that his coming be predicted or justified within the primary text of the Jewish people. As we will learn later on, this has become a big deal among those Christians in our time, and in many other times, who have wanted to convert Jews to Christianity.

It is important to remember that Jews should not refer to our Bible as the Old Testament, for that phrasing indicates that there is a Christian Scriptures. This becomes especially problematic when we remember that one of the translations of "testament" is "covenant," by which Christianity means to imply that the covenant between God and Israel (the Jewish people) has been replaced by the covenant given to the world with the coming of Jesus the Messiah. Instead we speak of the Jewish Bible as the תנך *Tanakh*, a Hebrew acronym made up of the first letters of the titles of the three parts of our Bible: Torah (ת), *N'vi'im*, or Prophets (נ) and *K'tuvim*, or "the writings" (כ). Or we simply call the Jewish Bible "our Bible."

As to institutional or structural issues of leadership, the simplest thing to say is that Christianity in general tends to be more hierarchical, meaning that there is a

Just who were THE Rabbis anyway? This is an important and complex question, especially in regard to this discussion, because THE Rabbis were pretty much the same guys with whom Jesus in New Testament stories seems to have a lot of conflict. Within this tension between Jesus and THE Rabbis you can see reflections of many of the differences between early Christianity and the Judaism of its time.

Generally speaking, THE Rabbis are understood to be the seventy men who constituted the Sanhedrin, or Rabbinic court, at the great Temple in Jerusalem, from about the second century B.C.E. until 70 C.E. when the Romans destroyed the Temple and exiled the Jewish people from Judea. (Obviously, as the years passed, the Sanhedrin was not always made up of the same seventy.) Interestingly enough, many of them were "part-timers" and actually had other jobs as well. THE Rabbis continued their work at their academies in Babylonia, which became the primary centers of Jewish life during the first centuries of the Diaspora. Their work as a distinct group continued until somewhere around the fifth century C.E. Over these many years they produced the great volumes of Jewish law and teaching: the Mishnah, the Talmud and the Midrash. THE Rabbis were teachers, scholars and judges; they served not only in Jerusalem, but also in local communities, and they had well-established traditions for how you got to become one of THEM. Jesus often referred to them as the Pharisees, but many scholars agree that it is not always clear exactly whom he meant.

The concept of seventy leaders is traced back to a famous story in the Torah, told in two different versions, in which Moses has to appoint seventy elders of the community to help him lead the Israelites. This relationship led to the subtle and important idea that Moses received the Torah directly from God and THE Rabbis (the seventy "little Moses") interpreted it from generation to generation.

definitive order of who's in charge and who is ultimately the boss. Judaism tends to be more democratic and consensus-driven. But let's be careful; this is not so in every case, or in every period of history, or in every denomination. We still have authoritative rabbis and dominant scholars, whereas at least some prominent Christian denomination have no professional clergy and is led entirely by lay people. But over all the tendency indicates that Christianity and Judaism favor different styles of leadership. On the third hand, as with many social issues in our time, things are changing right before our eyes with amazing speed.

The most familiar example of the Christian leadership tendency is within the largest Christian denomination, Catholicism. The Pope is an absolute authority with the final word on all issues of doctrine, belief and practice. He is advised to a certain degree by the Cardinals (not the St. Louis or Arizona type); but when he speaks it is as if the Church itself is speaking. This remarkable doctrine, called *ex cathedra* (from the chair), means that when the Pope declares he is speaking that way, he cannot make a mistake, ever. Christian tradition traces the authority of the Pope directly to Jesus, who said to his most favored disciple Peter, "You are Peter, and upon this rock I will build my church." As you will remember from Lesson 3, this is a pun on the Latin word *petra*, which means "rock", and it is why the Pope's church in Rome is called St. Peter's.

The large Orthodox churches of Greece and Russia have similar structures, but the various Protestant denominations have a wide range of leadership options, many of which were established in opposition to the Roman or Catholic style. You may find some very similar approaches within modern synagogues, mostly because Protestantism and the Judaism you experience began to flourish in modern Western civilization.

As we discussed in an earlier lesson, rabbis and other Jewish professionals are the primary authority figures of modern Judaism when it comes to our religious life. Historically rabbis have exercised much individual power and authority, not because they were brilliant speakers in the pulpit, but because they were insightful interpreters of what the Torah really meant to say. At many given moments in our history you could find one particular rabbi who might well be the most famous rabbi in the world and whose opinion was almost as important as the Pope's was to Catholics. Hillel and Maimonides are just two historic examples. But generally speaking, even those great rabbis, and others, have never had absolute authority; and controversies among our teachers have been the hallmark of Jewish life and, in many instances, the mechanisms by which we have changed and grown.

But ultimately the critical difference between Judaism and Christianity on the issue of authority might well be the issue of "creed" or "dogma". This is the concept that there is at least one clear and unequivocal belief without which you cannot be Christian or Jew. There is no such universally accepted religious dogma that has stood the test of time within Judaism. Maimonides came the closest with his "Thirteen Principles," but being Jews, we argued with him before the ink was even dry on the parchment.

It is so much the case that the only lasting definition of a Jew is the ethnic principle that "a Jew is someone born of a Jewish mother," and even this has been modified in contemporary, liberal Jewish life to include either parent as long as the child receives a Jewish

STATUE OF MAIMONIDES , CORDOBA, SPAIN
© PETER M. WILSON/CORBIS

TEXT OF MAIMONIDIES' THIRTEEN PRINCIPLES

"Ani Ma'amin"

1. I believe with perfect faith that God is the Creator and Ruler of all things.
2. I believe with perfect faith that God is One.
3. I believe with perfect faith that God does not have a body.
4. I believe with perfect faith that God is first and last.
5. I believe with perfect faith that it is proper to pray only to God.
6. I believe with perfect faith that all the words of the prophets are true.
7. I believe with perfect faith that the prophecy of Moses, the chief of all the prophets, is absolutely true.
8. I believe with perfect faith that the entire Torah that we now have is that which was given to Moses.
9. I believe with perfect faith that this Torah will not be changed, and that there will never be another given by God.
10. I believe with perfect faith that God knows all of man's deeds and thoughts.
11. I believe with perfect faith that God rewards those who keep His commandments, and punishes those who transgress them.
12. I believe with perfect faith in the coming of the Messiah.
13. I believe with perfect faith that the dead will be brought back to life when God wills it to happen.

Not too many years ago, a congregation of Jews who said that they did not believe in God, applied for membership in the Union for Reform Judaism, the national organization of Reform Jews. The application was discussed, as you might guess, with great passion and argument, and one of the issues was whether or not this community stepped outside the lines of some kind of Jewish "dogma", a place beyond which they could not go and still be a part of the national Jewish community. Ultimately, their application was rejected. What do you think? How would you have voted and why? Can you be Jewish and not believe in God, at least if you want to be a member of the Jewish "religious" community? What gives groups the power to make such decisions?

education and participates in acts of Jewish identification such as becoming bar or bat mitzvah.

Christianity is absolutely a dogmatic religion, and the basic dogma is the idea we looked at before: an absolute faith that Jesus is the Messiah, the son of God, both human and divine. Once again, without that belief you cannot be a Christian. While Jews might have some ideas we think are critical for us as individuals, there is still no comparable, universally accepted dogmatic statement for Jewish life. The lack of universal dogma is both a difficult complication (some of us love simplicity) and a blessing that causes us to challenge and re-invent ourselves as the world grows and changes (some of us love creativity).

About Celebrations and Rituals, Salvation and Social Responsibility

This one, thankfully, is almost easy to figure out. For all practical purposes, the vast majority of the celebrations and rituals that define Christianity are related to stories of the life of Jesus. From the baptism of small children and converts to Christmas and Easter, Christian observances are about the way in which the believer expresses his or her faith in the power of Jesus to bring salvation. Identifying one's own life with the life of Jesus is the Christian way of saying that one has faith in Jesus' ability to redeem him and the world.

In that regard the most important Christian holiday is Easter, the celebration of Jesus' resurrection, his return from death after the crucifixion. To say that Jesus is the Messiah is to say we can be redeemed from our sinfulness and saved from the punishment of eternal death in the same way that Jesus was. We can have life everlasting if we have faith in the truth of Jesus' resurrection and in the examples of his life story. There is no Christianity without the Easter story.

On the other hand, as we have said before, with the exception of Rosh ha-Shanah and Yom Kippur, most Jewish holidays are about the historic experiences of the entire Jewish people; most life-cycle celebrations are about the milestone experiences of our personal life and those of our family. Once again this happens because Judaism is defined as the religious expression of the Jewish *people*, and the ongoing covenantal dialogue between the children of Israel and God. It's one of the reasons, for example, that we have declared new Jewish religious observances such as *Yom ha-Atzma'ut* (Israeli Indepence Day) and *Yom ha-Shoah* (Holocaust Memorial Day).

In that same regard, the most important Jewish holiday is *Pesah*/Passover. As with Easter for Christians, there is no Judaism without the teachings and meanings of the Passover story for Jews. For Judaism, salvation is all about repairing the injustice of the world in which we live. We feel this strongly because once upon a time we were slaves in the land of Egypt, so we remember what it is to not be free and to suffer injustice. We "remember the heart of the stranger," is the most-often-repeated sentence in the Torah (35 times). It is not that Christianity doesn't also feel the impulse to social justice; it is simply a matter of emphasis and what experience is at the core of our identity. The core of Christian identity is Jesus' promise that we can escape eternal death and sinfulness if we believe in

JESUS FALLS AS HE CARRIES THE CROSS.

© DANIEL RADICEVIC

him; the core of Jewish identity is Passover's challenge to escape injustice.

But still we should say a word about Rosh ha-Shanah and Yom Kippur, the two non-historical holidays. They also represent a clear distinction between Judaism and Christianity as to the nature of sin and our ability to deal with it. Christianity, we noted in one of our earlier lessons, believes in the concept of original sin, the notion that sin is a basic part of the human condition (thanks to Adam), and that we can neither escape nor atone for it by ourselves. We need the help of our faith in Jesus. Judaism feels differently; we are not sinful by nature, and we can redeem ourselves through atonement, seeking and giving forgiveness. These are two radically different ways of looking at the nature of humanity. Rosh ha-Shanah and Yom Kippur celebrate the possibility of beginning again and of doing it by ourselves, with all the good intention and passion of our humanity. They are the High Holidays because if we observe them correctly, we feel really, really good when we have done our job.

Implicit in all of this is one of the great philosophical and religious differences between Judaism and Christianity, though once again it is a matter of degree, rather than exclusivity. **Christianity emphasizes faith; Judaism emphasizes deeds**. It is interesting to note that in many early parts of the Christian Scriptures Jesus urged his followers to obey the laws of the Torah, to be observant Jews. But after the Temple was destroyed by the Romans and the Jews were scattered throughout the world, Christianity turned to a new emphasis—faith in the life teachings of Jesus—an idea introduced by Paul. Because the Jews had rejected Jesus as Messiah, Christianity was reaching for a whole new audience, emphasizing a way of believing that could be accepted in a very different kind of world. Some scholars emphasize that for some the rule of the Roman Empire was oppressive, and many peoples lost hope of any relief in this world. Christianity, perhaps, offered them hope in another way and in another world. Judaism, on the other hand, flourished in Babylonia and discovered ways of surviving without being "at home." Judaism reemphasized *mitzvot*, or sacred works; Christianity developed the notion of having faith. This clear distinction between faith and works remains one of the most important issues to define our two religions.

So if, for example, you think about the Jewish life-cycle celebrations you know about, you can see clearly the way in which Judaism emphasizes deeds or works. When a baby is named, the wish is expressed that the child have a life filled with Torah, *huppah* and *ma'asim tovim*. Torah means learning, *huppah* (the marriage canopy) implies spending life with someone whom you love and

living responsibly within family and community. *Ma'asim tovim* means, quite literally, "doing good deeds." When you become bar or bat mitzvah you accept responsibility for the commandments, the things that a Jew is supposed to do. When you get married (*mazal tov!*) a glass is broken to remind you that the world is not whole, and that because two people love each other, they have the strength to help fix it. And when someone dies we do not celebrate a journey to heaven, where all will be well; instead we honor a life that left the world a better place than when it arrived. Life is really hard work, isn't it?

Obviously, there is much more to study in our comparisons of Judaism and Christianity. It is hoped that this will happen in your classroom discussions. What is always important to remember is that in our world, religious people—in fact, all decent people—should feel a responsibility to be respectful of the cherished beliefs and customs of one another. Religious passions go very deep, and we are all aware of the terrible things that can go wrong when we judge one another without information and perspective and tolerance. Let's not go down that road anymore!

Exercise

Here are two texts, one from the Torah and one from the Christian Scriptures. We are going to read and compare them.

Leviticus 19.32-37 YOU SHALL RISE UP BEFORE THE WHITE HEAD, AND HONOR THE FACE OF AN OLD MAN, AND YOU SHALL FEAR YOUR GOD: I AM THE ETERNAL. WHEN A STRANGER SOJOURNS WITH YOU IN YOUR LAND, YOU SHALL NOT WRONG HIM OR HER. THE STRANGER WHO LIVES WITH YOU SHALL BE TO YOU AS THE NATIVE AMONG YOU, AND YOU SHALL LOVE HIM AS YOURSELF; FOR YOU WERE STRANGERS IN THE LAND OF EGYPT: I AM THE ETERNAL, YOUR GOD. YOU SHALL DO NO WRONG IN JUDGMENT, IN MEASURES OF LENGTH OR WEIGHT OR VOLUME. YOU SHALL HAVE JUST BALANCES, JUST WEIGHTS...I AM THE ETERNAL YOUR GOD, WHO BROUGHT YOU OUT OF THE LAND OF EGYPT. AND YOU SHALL OBSERVE ALL MY STATUTES AND ALL MY ORDINANCES, AND DO THEM: I AM THE ETERNAL.

1. What does this text say is the heart of being a good Jew?

   _____

   _____

2. What lesson does it learn from the Egypt experience?

   _____

   _____

3. Why are little things like respect for the elderly and just weights mentioned as things that God wants you to do?

   _____

   _____

4. What does this text say about God?

   _____

   _____

JOHN 6.35-40 JESUS SAID TO THEM, "I AM THE BREAD OF LIFE; ONE WHO COMES TO ME SHALL NOT HUNGER, AND ONE WHO BELIEVES IN ME SHALL NEVER THIRST. BUT I SAID TO YOU THAT YOU HAVE SEEN ME AND YET DO NOT BELIEVE. ALL THAT THE FATHER GIVES ME WILL COME TO ME; AND ONE WHO COMES TO ME I WILL NOT CAST OUT. FOR I HAVE COME DOWN FROM HEAVEN, NOT TO DO MY OWN WILL, BUT THE WILL OF GOD WHO SENT ME; AND THIS IS THE WILL OF GOD WHO SENT ME, THAT I SHOULD LOSE NOTHING OF ALL THAT GOD HAS GIVEN ME, BUT RAISE IT UP AT THE LAST DAY. FOR THIS IS THE WILL OF MY FATHER, THAT EVERY ONE WHO SEES THE SON AND BELIEVES IN HIM SHOULD HAVE ETERNAL LIFE; AND I WILL RAISE THEM UP AT THE LAST DAY."

5. What does this text say is the essence of being a good Christian?

_____

_____

6. What is the relationship between the Father and the Son?

_____

_____

7. What does this text say about God?

_____

_____

8. What is the big difference between the two passages?

_____

_____

Chapter 5.
"Have You Accepted Our Lord Jesus?" Responding When Christian Missionaries Come to Call

Getting Ready

The follow quotation from the Christian Scriptures talks about the way that Paul went about selling Christianity to the world.

> **Corinthians 9.20-22**: To the Jews I became as a Jew, in order to win Jews; to those under the law I became as one under the law—though not being myself under the law—that I might win those under the law. To those outside the law I became as one outside the law—not being without law toward God but under the law of Christ—that I might win those outside the law. To the weak I became weak, that I might win the weak.

1. What does this passage teach about the way that some Christians view belief in Jesus?

   _____

   _____

2. Have you had experiences with Christians trying to influence your beliefs? What happened?

   _____

   _____

Hayyim ben Yehoshua begins an internet article by recalling the following being taught about Jesus at the Jewish day school he attended:

> "Jesus was a famous first century rabbi whose Hebrew name was Rabbi Yehoshua. His father was a carpenter named Joseph and his mother's name was Mary. Mary became pregnant before she married Joseph. Jesus was born in a stable in Bethlehem during a Roman census. Jesus grew up in Nazareth and became a learned rabbi. He traveled all over Israel preaching that people should love one another. Some people thought that he was the Messiah and he did not deny this, which made the other rabbis very angry. He caused so much controversy that the Roman governor Pontius Pilate had him crucified. He was buried in a tomb and later his body was found to be missing since it had probably been stolen by his disciples."

Refuting Missionaries, Hayyim ben Yehoshua, http://mama.indstate.edu/users/nizrael/jesusrefutation.html

3. What's wrong with this statement?

_____

_____

4. Why is it dangerous?

_____

_____

Christian Evangelism

You may have noticed lately that Christian evangelism is very big news—not only religious news but also political news. As social historians might say, right-wing Christians (the more conservative wing of American Christianity) have become prominently involved in American politics and in reaching out religiously to people like us who are not Christians. Especially people like us.

A WOMAN PRAYS AS SHE LISTENS TO BISHOP T.D. JAKES, PASTOR OF THE POTTER'S HOUSE CHURCH IN DALLAS, TEXAS, PREACH HIS MESSAGE.

© REUTERS/CORBIS

There are many reasons for these two efforts, but we are mostly concerned with the religious story. We want to know why it is that Christian evangelical movements are motivated to convert Jews to Christianity, how it is that they hope to do so and what you can do when they come to visit you. You may have noticed this in your schools in the various clubs and activities in which you participate and in your daily social encounters with your Christian friends and their families, mostly those who belong to various Protestant denominations.

Sometimes the Christian evangelical movement doesn't appear to be all that friendly. Some years ago a very large and very conservative church in our neighborhood organized a group of about thirty other congregations to join in a special outreach to local Jews. A large sum of money was collected, and a video about the life and teachings of Jesus was mailed to every Jewish home in our vicinity, targeted purposely to arrive just before the High Holidays! The accompanying literature was very explicit, talking of their love for Judaism and the Jewish people and expressing their concern for how much we were missing. Needless to say, our community was outraged at both the intent and the timing, and the effort was entirely without success and filled with bad feeling. Thankfully, many of the churches involved realized that they had not been told of the full plan, and they expressed their sincere apologies for something so hurtful at so important a time of the year.

So as we begin, please remember that this is not easy stuff, not simply because it involves a lot of history and philosophy, but because it may also involve your relationships with people who have been your friends for a very long time, and whose motives appear to be based in that friendship and their feelings for you. Let's try to conduct our discussions with respect for Christianity and its important contributions to the history of civilization and culture and religious teaching. But let's also be clear and proud of who we are and why we would like to stay that way. These attempts are not the work nor the active belief of most Christians, but they are getting more prominent, and it's necessary for us to be well prepared!

As we have learned, there are several important distinctions between Judaism and Christianity, and to varying degrees they are all a part of this particular discussion, too. So I hope you were paying attention. While some teachers have argued that the really important religious difference between the two religions (and also between some denominations within Christianity itself) is about faith and works, the key issue for wanting to convert Jews to Christianity is about the role of Jesus as Messiah. This is about the "good news" that belief in Jesus assures salvation at the time of his second coming. Evangelicals (check your vocabulary list) are people who want to spread that particular piece of "good news," and they want to do so because they really, really believe in it, and as your friend, they want you to share in it. So our job now will be to clarify again how what Jews believe is different and how we may respond, if we choose to do so (and whether we do respond is itself an important choice we have to make).

Even though it might appear that we Jews invented the concept of the Messiah, it is important to recognize how very little this idea is a part of who we are nowadays. Non-Orthodox Judaism does not believe in a personal Messiah, i.e. an *individual person* sent by God to save the Jews and the world from injustice and persecution. Traditional Orthodox Jews do believe in the coming of a personal

Messiah. For the most part, especially among non-Orthodox Jews, repairing the world is something we think God would like us to work at ourselves. (You may know this idea as *tikun olam*, the repair of the world.)

STORY TIME: To illustrate the notion that the coming of a Messiah-type-person is a distant matter, Jewish tradition records this story.

The residents of a small Jewish town were very concerned about one of their citizens who was very poor and whose family was always hungry. This poor man had absolutely no skills, so they couldn't imagine what kind of job he could hold that would support his family. They went to their rebbe and asked if he had any way of helping out this poor man and his family, and the rebbe said that, in fact, he had a good idea for a job. "We'll stand him at the edge of our town, and it will be his job to wait and watch for the Messiah. It doesn't require much skill, and best of all, it's a *permanent* position!"

(Get it?)

In a sense, Christianity does not believe in a personal Messiah either, but that's because their Messiah is not a "person" in the normal sense of an actual flesh-and-blood human being; their Messiah is Jesus, a human aspect of God's being. So while in many ways Messianism is not a big deal for Jews and Judaism (although there have been times in history when it has become more important), for Christians it is *the* big deal, and it is something that the missionary knocking on your door, or your head, would like you to know about.

ABOUT SOME SERIOUS JEWISH MESSIANISM: Every once in a while, especially when things were tough, Judaism did have some very involved Messianic ideas and some individual Jews who claimed that they were the Messiah, or whose followers claimed that this person was the Messiah. During the period of the Roman oppression, for example, many Jews thought that a guy named Bar Kokhba (Son of a Star…how's that for a Messianic name?) was the Messiah because he'd experienced good military success against the Romans.

Perhaps the most interesting Messianic pretender was a fellow named Shabbatai Zvi (1626-1676), who lived during a really bad time for the Jews in the Ottoman (Turkish) empire and in Poland and Russia as well. His appeal spread through those areas and into much of Western Europe. Scholars refer to the belief that he was the Messiah as the Sabbatean movement, and it was extremely powerful throughout the Jewish world of the 17th century.

This is a long and complicated story that is also involved with the Kabbalah (Jewish mysticism) and some of the really unusual ideas that it taught about the coming of the Messiah. One of those ideas is something called *Hevlai Mashiah*, the "birth pains of the Messiah."

This idea teaches that just as a woman gives birth to a child painfully, so does the world painfully "give birth" to the Messiah. The pain of the world is seen in such things as war, disease, poverty

71

and injustice, and the Kabbalah taught that when all of these horrible things were happening, the time was right for a Messiah to be born, just as it was in the time of Shabbatai Zvi.

Unfortunately, Mr. Zvi did not turn out to be much of a Messiah. In 1666 he was brought before the court of the Turkish Sultan, having been arrested, probably for something like inciting a rebellion. The Sultan offered him death or conversion to Islam, and he agreed to become a Muslim. Needless to say, this really upset the hundreds of thousands of Jews who viewed him as the Messiah, and it was the end of his claim and the movement. How about that?

PRAYING HANDS AT
ORAL ROBERTS UNIVERSITY IN
TULSA, OKLAHOMA.
© PHIL ANTHONY

Christian evangelicals believe that it is especially important to reach out to Jews on this issue for several reasons. In his time, we did not accept Jesus as the Messiah for many reasons, but mostly because he didn't really help us to free ourselves from the burden and sorrow of the Roman oppression of our people. An even more compelling issue for evangelical Christians, however, is their belief that our Bible (which they call the Old Testament) predicts the coming of Jesus the Messiah and that somehow we missed it! They are absolutely certain that the books of our Bible—the Torah, the Writings and the Prophets—have very clear messages that God will send His son to save us and the world. Our Bible is part of their Bible. The Old and the New Testament represent a seamless, continuing story, and it is amazing to proselytizers that we don't see what they see. Part of their task (a big part) is about teaching potential Jewish converts how to read our Bible in the same way that they do. Once you do so, you can't help but want to become a Christian.

There are some other issues that motivate the Evangelicals and dictate the content of what they say to you and the approaches they use. Some believe that Jesus will not return (and therefore Salvation is delayed) until his own people (that would be us) accept him. Others find it amazing that for two thousand years many peoples have tried to destroy us, but for some reason, as they view it, God must have wanted us to survive so that converted Jews will be around to welcome Jesus home. But the really powerful motivational issue remains this passion and responsibility that seems to come with knowing the news; evangelical Christians, *by definition*, are people who are supposed to convert the Jews. It's their job.

◆ ◆ ◆ ◆

For the most part, proselytizing Christians do their job with two different basic approaches. The first, as we've indicated, is rooted in their belief that this is an act of friendship and concern. They might begin with an innocent-sounding invitation to a dance or party at their church that seems to have nothing to do with religion. And truthfully, sometimes there's not much you can do about this other than say, "Thanks for your friendship and concern, but I'm doing just fine. I like who I am, I feel very strongly about what I believe in and I don't agree with what you believe in. A friend is someone who values me for what I am, not for the someone else they would like me to be. So let's just agree to see these things differently and get back to the music video we were watching in the first place." But, if they persist, you may have to limit your contact with them and, in the saddest case, end your friendship.

The other approach, as we've also said, is about text, and as difficult as ending a friendship may be, this response also requires careful study, argumentation and detailed preparedness. It also requires you to be thoughtful and articulate and calm in your discussion with Christian proselytizers. So if you're not ready to do all of the prep work, you may want to think very carefully about just closing the door when they come to call (no slamming allowed). If you try to play the text game and you're not trained and ready, just like in sports, you could lose, and that would be, many smart people think, a tragedy for you, your family and the Jewish people. So let's be sure we understand how this game works before you decide if this is what you're ready to do.

The text game, one more time, is based upon the Christian belief that our Bible, which they call the Old Testament, predicts the important teachings and stories of the New Testament. If you accept the "Old" Testament, as they see it, you also have to accept the teachings of the "New". All they have to do, then, is convince you that what you are reading in certain passages of our Bible is about Jesus as Messiah. Your job, in playing this game, is to have enough information to respond accurately that there is no way in the world that that could be the case; and in all cases, smart Jewish people have been able to show that that is so. But it is a lot of work, and unless you're able and willing to do all of this, it may not be the best idea for you.

One of the most famous examples is a reference in the prophet Isaiah, Chapter 7:14. In the authoritative Christian translation of the Hebrew, as first translated from the Greek, the verse says, "Behold a virgin shall conceive and bear a son, and shall call his name Immanuel." (The authoritative translation in the *Jewish* version from the Jewish Publication Society is "Behold the young woman shall conceive and bear a son and shall call his name Immanuel.")

Needless to say, you should be able to figure out where this is going!

But there is absolutely no scholarly doubt that Isaiah was not telling King Ahaz in 734 B.C.E. that in seven centuries from *then*, Jesus was going to be born and save Jerusalem from the two enemy armies that are *at that moment in 734 B.C.E.* besieging the capital city. That is the actual context of the verse, and scholars have made very clear what Isaiah is saying, in Hebrew and in content, is something entirely different. First of all, the Hebrew word a*lmah* does not mean "virgin"; it means a young woman old enough to be married. On top of that, Hebrew grammarians will tell you that the tense of the Hebrew verb is not really about the distant future, but about the very near or foreseeable future. On top of that, Isaiah does not say **a** young woman but **the** young woman; most scholars assume that to either mean someone he knows or King Ahaz knows. On top of that, consider Isaiah's purpose: He is trying to calm the king's anxiety over his current enemies outside the gates of Jerusalem. Why would he be talking about an event still many centuries away, and why would he call the kid Immanuel and not Jesus? He's trying to say to Ahaz, "Don't worry, your relief will come relatively soon. The birth of a child with this name assures that there *is* a future and that God is on our side."

That's how you can respond to the text game effectively, but as you can see, you really gotta know your stuff, and you should also have the time and the place and the frame of mind to do this appropriately. And you should demand that the evangelizer have the frame of mind to listen respectfully to you. (By the way, I am very grateful to have heard a lecture by Dr. Michael Cook of the Hebrew Union College in which these responses were put forth in the articulate and careful manner I have tried to reproduce here.)

There are many, many other examples of these kinds of verses proselytizers may call "proof texts" to prove the predictions of Jesus they say are in our Bible. Many of them come from the prophetic books, such as Isaiah, Hosea and Zechariah. Then there's a whole bunch of them in the book of Daniel that are used as important references in the Christian Scriptures Book of Revelation. (As it turns out, the texts in Daniel are probably about the <u>Hanukkah</u> story and not Jesus.) Believe me, there are very good refutations of all of these texts, but I'll bet that many of you haven't even read some of these books just for their Jewish importance! So once

A JEWS FOR JESUS PREACHER HOLDING THE BIBLE OUTSIDE THE OFFICIAL CEREMONIES AT GROUND ZERO.

again, if an evangelizer does know all of this stuff, he or she might have little trouble convincing you of its truth. Just be careful and, if you need, ask for help from your rabbi, educator, teacher or other knowledgeable Jewish people you know.

What can you do effectively at the moment you are approached? Be polite, but make it very clear that you're not interested. Explain to the person that you understand that this is his job, but that you also have a job to do, and that is to enjoy the very special fulfillment you can find from being Jewish. Who knows? Maybe you can get one of them to join us. (Just kidding!) And if, unfortunately, you are angry about some Jewish *mishegass* that your parents or teachers have bothered you about, this is not the way to get your revenge. You can cause permanent damage in attempting to relieve what is a very temporary situation. In other words, don't take de bait unless you can do the debate.

Finally, most of this happens to kids who are in high school, and it often happens with kids who are seen as vulnerable and lonely. You might need to be a friend to another Jewish kid who is struggling with certain kinds of identity issues. At the extreme end of these issues there have been problems with cults and kidnappings, but thanks to a large-scale response in most Jewish communities with cooperation from Christian friends, some of the really bad stuff has disappeared. There are some very effective Jewish organizations working in our communities, and someone at your synagogue may help you or your family find them if the need should arise. Just don't think that this could never happen to you or to someone you know; try to be a Torah for yourself, your family and your friends.

Case Study

Nathan and Temima Feldman came to Denver's Orthodox Jewish community, a youthful couple professing a search for deeper, more meaningful Judaism, evincing a commitment to the radical lifestyle changes that come with the decision to live according to Jewish law, or *halakhah*. They were duly welcomed as such, with open arms, and helped considerably along their way by a community that prides itself on openness and support for those who wish to join its ranks. Within months the Feldmans became active participants in the religious and social life of that community, celebrating a wedding in the Orthodox custom, having a *bris* for their infant son, adopting the dress and mannerisms of Torah-observant Jews, avidly studying Torah and other Jewish subjects, working and volunteering for several Orthodox institutions, living in the homes of Denver Jews and apparently establishing close friendships with members of the community.

TWO INDIVIDUALS FROM THE ORGANIZATION JEWS FOR JESUS HAND OUT PAMPHLETS TO PEDESTRIANS.

© JACQUES M. CHENET/CORBIS

Ultimately they applied for *aliyah* under Israel's Law of Return and were initially accepted by Israeli immigration authorities, who based their decision on the recommendations of two Denver Orthodox rabbis. But the *aliyah* was halted suddenly earlier this month—as well as the Feldman's most unusual sojourn in the Jewish community—when it was discovered that the Feldmans are not Jewish at all, and in fact have close personal ties to a Messianic, Hebrew-Christian congregation in Ft. Collins. The discovery sent shock waves of apprehension and distrust through the Orthodox community of Denver.

REPRINTED FROM *THE INTERMOUNTAIN JEWISH NEWS.* BY CHRIS LEPPEK, IJN ASSISTANT EDITOR

1. Why would Christian missionaries pretend to be observant Jews? What do they have to gain?

2. How should Jews tell the difference between Christians and Jews who are sincerely interested in becoming more Jewish or learning more about Judaism and those who have an agenda?

3. How can Jews protect themselves from missionaries?

Proselytizing Questions and Smart Jewish Answers

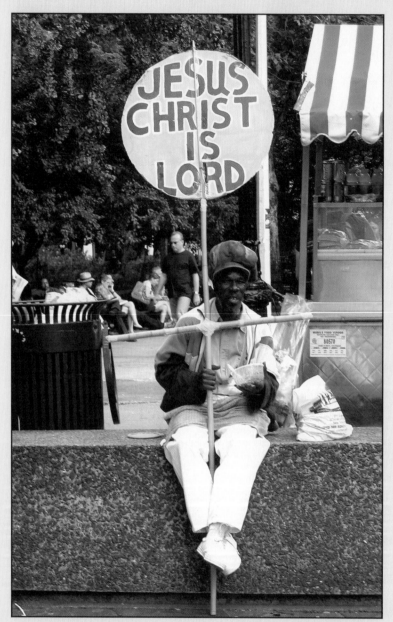

© RICHARD KERSHAW

Q1: Have you accepted our Lord Jesus Christ?

A1: "No, why should I?" (While this answer might seem on the surface to invite a response and further debate, the issue is about burden of proof. There might be better wording that will end the exchange more quickly, but it needs to be clear that it is not my job to prove the proselytizer wrong; it is up to him/her to make the case.)

Q2: Wouldn't you like to be saved from death and eternal damnation?

A2: "For me as a Jew, salvation is not about relief from death. Judaism teaches that death is the enemy, not something to be looked forward to, nor a transition to some better place. I believe that salvation means being saved from injustice and saving others from that fate as well. Death is inevitable, heaven is unprovable, and as for me, I save at the First National Bank.

Q3: Did you know that many texts in your own Bible predict and prove the coming of Jesus as Messiah?

A3: First of all, it's not likely, say Jewish scholars, that biblical Judaism had any kind of Messianic ideas whatsoever. And this Bible of ours was written, for the most part, many hundreds of years before Jesus and deals with the lives and beliefs of the Israelites in their own time. You, my friend, are reading biblical stories through the eyes of much later history and trying to make it look as if our Bible does what you wish it had.

Q4: Jesus died for your sins. His death is automatic atonement for all the bad stuff you do, and he thereby grants you pretty easy, vicarious atonement. Doesn't that sound like a good offer?

A4: Jesus didn't die for my sins; he doesn't even know me. Besides, as I understand what it means to be a human being, I am perfectly capable of atoning all by myself. In fact, I like it that way; it teaches me a sense of responsibility for myself and the world in which I live, and it's healthy to confront the reality of our own lives and deal with it. Judaism and Christianity have different views of the capabilities of human beings; it's kind of summed up in the difference between original sin, over which we have no control, and being just plain human. I like that Judaism has much more faith in me and my own strength.

Q5: Did you know that the Christian covenant with God replaces that of the Israelites? We are the new Israel.

A5: Says who? You just proclaimed yourselves to be that, and you didn't even have a big ceremony with thunder and lightning like at Mt. Sinai. The Bible describes our covenant with God as everlasting, and even though the biblical God gets a little angry at times and wants out of the deal, it never really happens. The prophet Isaiah teaches us that as long as we (the Jews) bear witness to God's holiness, then the nations will know that God is indeed God. In other words, God needs us just as much as we need God…and I like the sense of partnership and responsibility. Your claim is just like that of a third party who sees that two friends have a really good relationship and tries to move in on the deal. Eventually that third party gets really angry that the other two aren't paying all that much attention to him, and so he makes all kinds of silly claims that just aren't so.

Chapter 6.
An Introduction to Islam
Some History, Some Vocabulary and a Few of Its Most Important Ideas

First Thought

In the Qu'ran the Muslims are instructed to say:

> We believe in God, and that which has been sent down on us, and sent down on Abraham and Ishmael, Isaac and Jacob, and the Tribes, and in that which was given to Moses and Jesus, and the prophets, of the Eternal; we make no division between distinction among any of them, and to Allah we surrender. *Surah III (1)*

1. What things are surprising in this passage?
2. How is it different from a Jewish prayer?
3. What does it teach about the relationship between Islam, Judaism and Christianity?

The Sacrifice of Isaac/ Ishmael

The Qu'ran (the sacred text and basic revelation of Islam) and the Torah tell the same story with some interesting differences.

Torah

> **Genesis 22:1–2.** After these things God tested Abraham and said to him: "Abraham." He said: "Hineini (meaning I am here)." God said: "Please take your son, your only one, the one you love, Isaac, and take yourself to the land

SACRIFICE OF ISAAC BY ANTON PAVLOVIC LOSENKO
© THE STATE RUSSIAN MUSEUM/CORBIS

of Moriah (meaning seeing) and offer him as a sacrifice upon one of the mountains that I will tell you."

Genesis 22:10–12. Abraham sent out his hand to take the knife to kill his son. An angel of Adonai called to him from above: "Abraham, Abraham." He said: "Hineini." The answer came: "Don't send out your hand to the boy. Don't do anything to him at all, because now I know that you are in awe of God. You didn't hold back your son, your only one, from Me."

Qu'ran

APPEARANCE OF THE ANGEL TO HAGAR AND ISHMAEL BY GIOVANNI BATTISTA TIEPOLO FROM FRESCO CYCLE DEPICTING SCENES FROM THE OLD TESTAMENT
© ELIO CIOL/CORBIS

He said: "I will go to my God! God will surely guide me. O my God! Grant me a righteous son!" So, We gave him the good news of a coming son. Then, when the son reached the age of serious work with him, he said: "O my son! I have seen in a vision that I offer you in sacrifice…" The son said: "O my father! Do as you are commanded: you will find me, if Allah so wills, one of the steadfast!" So when they had both submitted to Allah, and he had laid him prostrate on his forehead for sacrifice, We called out to him "O Abraham!…Thou hast already fulfilled the vision!"—thus indeed do We reward those who do right. (37.99–109)

4. How are these stories similar?

5. How are these stories different?

6. How is God different in each story?

7. Who is telling the second story?

8. Who is the son in the first story?

9. Who is the son in the second story?

The Opinion of Ibn Kathîr

As is often the case with the Torah, one can't understand the Qu'ran without a commentary.

"SO WE GAVE HIM THE GOOD NEWS OF A COMING SON."

READING FROM A QU'RAN
© WAEL HAMDAN

And this son is Ishmael, for he is the first son whose good news was brought to Abraham. He is older than Isaac, according to Muslims, and *ahl al-kitâb* (i.e., the People of the Book), too. It is even said in their Scripture that Ishmael was born when Abraham was eighty-six years old and Isaac was born when Abraham was ninety-nine. In their Scripture as well, God is said to have ordered Abraham to sacrifice his **only son**, and in another version his **firstborn**. And at this spot they inserted falsely the name of Isaac against the text of their very Scripture. The reason they inserted Isaac is that he is their father, whereas Ishmael is the father of the Arabs. They added Isaac out of envy and brushed away "**only son**" by saying that Ishmael and his mother had already been to Mecca.

10. How does this commentary solve the son problem?

11. Where is the Qu'ran right about the Torah, and where is it wrong?

12. What does this commentary reveal about the relationship between Islam and Judaism?

Hebrew and Arabic

One of the first things you may notice as we begin our study of Islam is that some of its Arabic vocabulary sounds a little bit familiar to you. That's because Hebrew and Arabic grew up in the same part of the world, just as European languages (and English) share a common denominator of Latin roots and geographic proximity. For example, the word **ISLAM** itself is clearly related to the Hebrew word *shalom*, and in that relationship we can find one of the first connections between these two great religions.

Islam is usually translated by Muslim scholars (in a minute we'll talk about the word Muslim, too), as "submission". But it specifically means a *peaceful* submission to the will of **ALLAH**, or God, a submission that brings *peace* to the believer. (I hope you also noticed that Allah sounds a little bit like *Elohim*.) So, Islam is the name of the religion, and a **Muslim** (same root letters) is a person who accepts the beliefs of Islam, who peacefully submits to the will of Allah and follows the teachings, traditions and practices first developed by **MOHAMMED**, the primary prophet of Islam. (However, the word Muslim is also often used as an adjective for countries or institutions within the Muslim community, e.g., that's a Muslim state.)

These teachings of Mohammed were first written in the **QU'RAN**, the holy book of Islam, supposedly dictated to him by the angel Gabriel. Mohammed lived from 570 C.E. to 632 C.E. He was born in the Muslim holy city of **MECCA** in the southern part of Saudi Arabia. (That's why it's a holy city for Islam.) The experiences of his life and the content of the revelation he received constitute the essence of Islam, together with the interpretations and commentaries of many later teachers.

Today more than one billion Muslims are scattered throughout the world. Contrary to what most of you probably think, a very large percentage of Muslims live outside of the Middle East, speak little if any Arabic and live relatively normal lives within their various countries. The largest population of Muslims lives in Indonesia. If present rates of growth continue, soon there may very well be more Muslims in the United States than Jews. Islam is the second largest religion in Europe. Jerusalem is the third holiest city for Muslims. As

THE 27TH OF RAMADAN, *LAYLET AL-QADR* (NIGHT OF POWER), IS ONE OF THE HOLIEST NIGHTS OF THE ISLAMIC CALENDAR, THE NIGHT WHEN THE QU'RAN BEGAN TO BE REVEALED TO THE PROPHET MUHAMMAD. ALMOST ONE MILLION PILGRIMS VISIT MECCA FROM ALL OVER THE WORLD AND PRAY OVER THE NIGHT.

© AYAZAD

you may have heard, there are several different denominations within Islam, and as in Iraq, they don't always get along well. In many Arabic countries Muslims also control the government, and in parts of Africa, Europe and, of course, the Middle East there have been conflicts between Muslims, Christians and secular governments for control. Some Muslim denominations are very militant and critical of Western civilization, and much of that is part of what we are experiencing now in our world.

Mohammed and Mecca

As mentioned before, in Mecca, at the age of forty in 610 C.E., Mohammed was given a revelation from Allah through the angel Gabriel. It is addressed "to Humanity." A second revelation followed, some years later, in the city of Medina. According to some scholars, there is a marked difference in the tone of the two revelations. Over time these messages were transcribed and collected into what became the Qu'ran, though it was not completed until 652. Gabriel told him to preach the content of what he had heard to the warring tribes of Mecca and the Arabian Peninsula; it might unify them. These messages, in fact, eventually did just that. They also influenced Mohammed's views on other religions of the area, and from there he spread the influence of Islam into much of the world. This influence was not always attained peacefully, and in the Middle Ages Islam became the dominant religion and political power of the Middle East, as well as in Northern Africa and some parts of Mediterranean Europe. In many places the Muslim conquest of these areas had a remarkably positive influence and legacy.

In the two centuries after Mohammed's death in 632 C.E. the Arabs from Medina and throughout Arabia launched an incredibly successful military campaign that conquered most of Byzantium, Persia, North Africa, Turkey and Spain—in short, most of the Mediterranean world. At the same time that the Muslims were conquering these lands, their teachers and scholars were developing what Islam was to be; and at the same time as they were doing that, the Jews of Arabia were exchanging elements of their culture and belief with Islam. (One of the most fascinating examples of this interchange is the development of the centrality of Abraham and Ishmael in Islamic belief.) But despite this ongoing exchange, the Muslims never succeeded in converting the Jewish communities they encountered. In fact, throughout the Islamic conquest Jews were often given a special status in which they were called *dhimmi*, protected subjects. And interestingly enough, throughout the newly acquired Muslim lands Jews were provided relief from what had been a painful persecution by various Christian regimes in which they lived.

In this "Golden Age" of Islam the Muslim empire far outshone the Christian world of Europe, which, as you may know, was in what we often refer to as its "Dark Age". Spain under Muslim rule, in particular, was a rich world of art and literature, poetry and philosophy. One writer has said that the Jews of the Muslim world of this time (roughly from the 8th to the 13th century) were the world's leading Jews, just as the Islamic world was far superior to all of Europe in many endeavors. In wealth and culture, in religious and intellectual achievement, this was certainly one of the most productive and influential eras in all of Jewish history—especially in Spain, but also, for example, in what is now Iraq. It would take the Reformation and Renaissance to rebuild the centrality of European culture, and the Crusades to drive Islamic rule from the Holy Land. And neither the Crusades nor the Inquisition of reconquered Spain were "good for the Jews."

As protected subjects of the Islamic world of Spain and North Africa, Jewish life flourished in many different ways, and the academies and schools of Iraq re-energized Jewish religious teaching. In Spain Jews lived in self-governing communities that regulated all of Jewish life and exchanged official communication with the

As Mohammed's prophecies began to take hold in the Arab world, pagan opposition in Mecca forced him to flee to the city of Medina. In this large agricultural capital his teachings flourished, and Islam began to enter a larger world. In Medina there also lived a sizable Jewish population, Arabian Jews who were well integrated into the larger community, who spoke Arabic and were quite familiar with the traditions of their Arab neighbors. They also developed a kind of Jewish dialect of Arabic, in the same way that Yiddish was a combination of German and Hebrew, and Ladino a combination of Spanish and Hebrew. No one really knows for sure where these Arabian Jews came from, but it is clear that it was in Medina that the complex relationship between Judaism and Islam, Muslims and Jews began, and it was here that the "Golden Age of Islam" began within which there was to come the "Golden Age of Spanish Jewry".

Muslim rulers. Great philosophers and scholars such as Bahya Ibn Pakuda, Abraham Ibn Ezra, Saadia Gaon, Maimonides, Gersonides and David Kim<u>h</u>i elevated the world of Jewish scholarship. (They were often influenced by Muslim philosophers, as well as by Aristotle and the ancient Greeks.) Remarkable poetic literature was produced by such artists as Solomon Ibn Gabirol and Judah Ha-Levi. Jews served in the Muslim court. The poet Ibn Gabirol was also a general in the army of the Muslim Caliph. And while this world was not without tension between the two communities, it was a time of unparalleled accomplishment and prosperity for our people, and certainly one of the most influential times in the development of Jewish thought, culture, literature and art—and all under Islamic rule.

THE PROPHET'S MOSQUE (MASJID NABAWI), WAS FIRST BUILT IN THE YEAR 622 C.E. THE WALLS WERE MADE OF MUD BRICKS AND THE ROOFS WERE SUPPORTED BY TRUNKS OF PALM TREES.

© AYAZAD

In one story told in the Qu'ran, Gabriel took Mohammed on a journey to Jerusalem, and from the spot where the Dome of the Rock now stands he was taken up to meet Abraham, Moses and Jesus and lead them in prayer. In another revelation in the Qu'ran, Mohammed was taught the importance of Mecca as the place from which God instructed Abraham to sacrifice his son Ishmael—not Be'er Sheva and not Isaac. (Islamic tradition believes Ishmael to be the father of the Arab peoples.) To some extent we can understand these ideas as part of an original Islamic belief that all of Mohammed's predecessors were really Muslims and that Islam is meant to incorporate and honor the right teachings from them but also now takes their place as the One Right Way.

Unfortunately, during the early medieval ages this view often lead to violent conquest. The concept of **JIHAD**, commonly translated as "holy war", was introduced to justify the attempt to spread Islam and to motivate those who fought on its behalf. Later in his life while he was living in the city of Medina, Mohammed developed a "political" constitution for Islam in which the tribes of Arabia were united into the community of Islam and became what we call a theocratic state—a state for all practical purposes ruled by the will of God as made clear in the Qu'ran. These laws compose the **SHARIA**, the legal code of Islam. It is for this reason that we see to this very day the close association between religious and political leaders in many Muslim countries; it is becoming common knowledge that the **AYATOLLAH** in any country is usually more important and more influential than any political leader. This is a structure that is very different from what we know in the United States and much of Western civilization, where religion and state are clearly separated.

JERUSALEM
©AVNER RICHARD

◆　◆　◆　◆

As Islam developed from the original teachings of Mohammed, its religious principles developed into a complex system of beliefs and behaviors, just like the history of Judaism and Christianity. As with many religions, different denominations of Islamic belief developed; you have probably heard of Shi'ites and Sunnis. Despite these various views and sometimes geographic, national or politi-

An ayatollah is often the supreme religious leader of a large region or even an entire country; you have probably heard references to the recent "Supreme Leader" of Iran, the Ayatollah Khomeini, whose power was greater than that of the president of the country. Usually no political leader of a Muslim state would do anything without consulting the ayatollah. In local congregations and mosques the leader is usually referred to as the imam; he functions somewhat like a priest, minister or rabbi and seldom exercises any political power. His authority is based on his knowledge of Islam. This is the sort of Muslim leader you would most commonly encounter in the United States.

cal differences, for the most part we can conclude that there are six major areas of belief important to all of Islam: **MONOTHEISM, ANGELS, PROPHETS, SACRED TEXT, JUDGMENT, PARADISE** and **HELL**. In terms of their importance, they are roughly equivalent to the **CORE IDEAS** we have identified in Judaism and Christianity, and we will look at them next. There are also, of course, holidays and special observances, personal religious practices, worship services, a structure of authority and leaders, and all of the outward behaviors and customs that reflect the content within these areas of belief. These were developed over many centuries and often represent the face of Islam that many people see. So now, as we look at the big ideas and beliefs of Islam, we'll review some of the vocabulary we've talked about so far and a few new additions as well, especially some words and ideas you may have encountered in the news.

Muslim Belief

Any observant, devout Muslim will tell you that all of Islam is summarized and contained within its basic creedal statement, often referred to as the great confession, the **SHAHADA.** It is spoken in Arabic "*Ilaha illa Allah. Muhammad rasul Allah,*" and in English it translates to "**There is no god but Allah. Muhammad is the messenger of God.**" For all practical purposes, Muslims believe that to say these words, and mean them when you say them, is to convert to Islam, and that to say them is what makes a Muslim a Muslim. It is clearly understood that within the acceptance and repetition of these words is an acknowledgment of the various other beliefs that make the religion. *That's it!* But you can't go home just yet.

Muslim belief is expressed in the six areas that we mentioned a little earlier, but it is also lived through a vast culture of behaviors, traditions and customs, holidays and personal practices. There's a lot going on in the everyday life of a Muslim and an Islamic community (observant Muslims pray five times every day), and most of that is much more than we can handle here. But for now, let's concentrate on the ideas and beliefs that are contained and expressed in that six-word creed, and in our next lesson we'll compare them to Judaism.

Muslims, like Jews and Christians, are **MONOTHEISTS**. they have a belief in one God and one God only. Before Mohammed came along, the Arabic tribes worshipped many different gods, and it was Mohammed's teaching that unified them in the worship of **ALLAH**. In the Qu'ran Mohammed most commonly expresses one of the names of Allah as Ra<u>h</u>man, the Merciful One. Islam says that God is One, and God is also what the philosophers call "transcendent".

The concept of transcendence implies that Allah is over and above everything else and therefore cannot really be part of creation as we know it. God cannot be anything in this world or even similar to anything in this world. We cannot even know the real nature of God's being, though thanks to prophets like Mohammed who receive God's message, we can know what God would like us to do. This is a major Muslim idea; as one scholar has written, "God reveals His law, but does not reveal Himself." Remember that!

Therefore **ANGELS** are important to Islam. They are invisible spiritual beings who carry out God's commands and deliver certain messages. Some of them have particular job descriptions, such as the Angel Michael, who is the guardian of the Jews. There is a unique Muslim tradition that two angels are assigned to each of us (if we are Muslims) when we are born, and during our lifetime one of them records all of our good deeds and the other all of our bad deeds. If you were a Muslim, you would want to get to know these two, because their record-keeping will determine how you do on Judgment Day.

PROPHETS, on the other hand, are people; they have been sent to deliver God's message, and for the most part, Islam accepts the teachings of the major prophets of Judaism and Christianity. Islam is especially fond of Abraham and Jesus, but it is also careful to say that Jesus is not God or the Son of God; only Allah can be God. Though there is an Islamic tradition that recognizes some 124,000 prophets throughout previous history, the Big Six other than Mohammed himself are Abraham, Ishmael, Isaac, Jacob, Moses and Jesus.

Though Muslims believe in most parts of the ancient books of Judaism and Christianity, they also believe that these books and scrolls have become corrupted, mis-interpreted and re-inter-preted time and time again. Nor are there any original texts remain-ing to indicate what they might have said when they were pure. As a result, for Islam only the Qu'ran is complete, without error and perfectly clear. It is the unquestioned and perfect word of God. It is, as we sometimes say, "the last word". While the Qu'ran is not exactly Allah Himself, Muslims do believe that if a person should say something unpleasant about the Qu'ran, he or she is also saying something unpleasant about God. It is the standard for all truth, and if another sacred text agrees with the Qu'ran, it is also sacred; but if it disagrees, guess what! In this world, special rec-ognition and status are given to those scholars who memorize the entire 77,394 words of the Qu'ran, and when the Day of Judgment comes, this person, called a **HAFIZ,** is given double goodies in the next world.

The most important Islamic prayer, used dur-ing the five daily prayer services, summarizes what Muslims believe about God. It is called the Fatiha: "In the name of Allah, Most Gracious, Most Merciful. Praise be to Allah the Cherisher and Sustainer of the Worlds. Most Gracious, Most Merciful, Master of the Day of Judgment. You do we worship, and Your aid we seek. Show us the straight way, the way of those on whom Thou has vested Your grace, those whose portion is not anger and who will not go astray."

Which brings us, conveniently enough, to Islam's thoughts about **JUDGMENT DAY** and the life to come. Islam is very clear: One of these days this world is going to end with great calamity and destruction. The Qu'ran describes all of the signs of its imminent arrival; that world is not a very nice place in which to live, and it comes quickly to its end with all kinds of unimaginable disasters.

And then both the living and the dead will be called to judgment at individual "trials". Apparently, nothing happens to you immediately after you die; everything that is going to happen waits for this final Day of Judgment.

So don't forget about those two angels who are keeping copious notes on all the stuff you did, for those records will be read and will determine if you wind up in Heaven or Hell. There are very complete descriptions of these two options, but Muslim scholars insist that they not be taken literally, since no one alive has ever really seen them. Perhaps they are only meant to make you consider carefully what you're doing...or not doing, as is the case in many religious systems. Whatever it is, if I were you and you were me, and we were Muslims, we'd go for the Paradise Package. Paradise is a beautiful garden with magnificent flowing streams of pure water, rivers of milk, fountains of honey and oases filled with fresh fruit. There are delights for each of the senses and (**PG-13 alert!!**), for men only (especially soldiers) there are seventy-two beautiful virgins each. Hell, on the other hand, is not something you want to read about. The Qu'ran is horribly graphic in its description of Hell; nobody would want to go there, so why would you even think about behaving in the way that would send you there?

Implicit in these promises is the Islamic belief that we are each responsible for our own behavior, and we are perfectly free to choose what we will. Islam does not accept the notion of Original Sin. No one else can accept responsibility for what we do, and vice versa, and no one can save you from the choices you made except for yourself. But even though Islam disagrees with two of the most important teachings of Christianity (remember those?), Muslim leaders would want you to know of their admiration and reverence for Jesus as a prophet of God.

Finally, Islam has relatively little to say specifically about the concept we have discussed called **SALVATION**. What it does say that we can use for any comparative discussion is that something will happen after the Day of Judgment, and everyone will be resurrected (brought back from death to some form of life) in order to live in either Heaven or Hell. The world as we know it no longer exists; there is only Paradise or Hell.

Muslim Practice

These are the basic beliefs, the big ideas of Islam. Once again, there is so much yet to be explored about the customs and ceremonies, the traditions and holidays common in every Islamic community, though perhaps slightly different from one part of the world to the other. For example, like Jews, Muslims have particular traditions about food and fasting; there are celebrations common to all Muslims and also many local or regional events. In your lives, I suppose, you know much more about Christianity than Islam—at least you can name major Christian holidays—but I'll bet that isn't so for Islam.

Perhaps you'll have an opportunity to learn some of those things, too. Today we are in the business of comparing ideas and beliefs, and that will be our next item of business.

MUSLIM MAJOR HOLIDAY CALENDAR

THE MONTHS OF THE YEAR ARE:

Muharram	Jamadi I	Ramadan
Safar	Jamadi II	Shawwal
Rabi'I	Rajab	Dhu al Qu'da
Rabi"II	Shaban	Dhu al Hijjah

HOLIDAYS ARE:

First of Muharram:	The New Year
Tenth of Muharram:	Ashura is a fast day observing the assassination of Hussein, the grandson of Mohammed.
Twelfth of Rabi'I:	The birthday of Mohammed.
Twenty-seventh of Rajab:	The night when Mohammed was taken on a winged animal from Mecca to Jerusalem. He met with Jesus and then was taken back to Mecca.
Fourteenth of Shaban:	A night of repentance on which God descends to the lowest heavens to call to Muslims and grant forgiveness.
Ramadan:	Muslims fast from sunrise to sunset for the entire month.
Twenty-seventh of Ramadan:	Commemorating the time when Gabriel brought the first revelation to Mohammed.
First of Shawwal:	The day after the fasting of Ramadan ends, a happy festival called *Id Fitr* breaks the fast. It is a very happy, festive holiday.
Dhu al Hijjah 1-10:	The time of the Hajj, the pilgrimage to Mecca required of all Muslims once in their lifetime. (The focal point of the Haj is the Ka'ba stone marking the place, according to Muslim tradition, where Abraham offered to sacrifice his son Ishmael.)
Tenth of Dhu al Hijjah:	A festival observing the conclusion of the Hajj.

AN INDONESIAN MUSLIM WOMAN WEARING AN ARABIC HEADBAND THAT READS "THERE IS NO GOD BUT ALLAH".
© REUTERS/BEAWIHARTA

Exercise

Take a look at this passage from the Qu'ran. It speaks about Islamic belief.

> Allah! There is no god but Allah, the Living, the Self-Sustaining, the Supporter of all. It is Allah who sent down to you step by step, in truth, this Book, confirming what went before it; and Allah sent down the Torah (of Moses) and the Gospel (of Jesus) before this, as a guide to humankind, and Allah sent down the Qu'ran of judgment between right and wrong.
>
> Then those who reject faith in the signs of Allah will suffer the severest criticism and Allah is exalted in Might, Lord of Retribution. From Allah, verily nothing is hidden, on earth or in the heavens. (Qu'ran, Surat 3, vv. 1-5)

1. What does this text say about the Jewish and Christian Bibles?
2. How does it compare the Qu'ran to the Torah and the Gospels?
3. What does this passage say about belief in Allah?

Here is another passage that compares the Torah and the Gospels to the Qu'ran.

> Ye People of the Book (Jews)! Why do you dispute about Abraham, when the Torah and the Gospel were not revealed till after him? Have ye no understanding?
>
> Ah! You are those who fell to disputing even in matters of which you had some knowledge. But why dispute you in matters of which you have no knowledge? It is Allah who knows and you know not!
>
> Abraham was not a Jew nor yet a Christian: But he was upright and bowed his will to Allah's (which is Islam) and he joined not God with Allah. (Qu'ran, Surat 3, vv .65-67)

4. What is the Qu'ran's complaint about the Torah (and the Gospels)?
5. What does the Qu'ran claim is the truth about Abraham?
6. What is the meaning of "and he joined not God with Allah"?

Basic Islam

To conclude, use this chapter and fill in the following categories:

1. **GOD AND FAITH** (Who is the God, and what are you supposed to believe?)

   _____

   _____

   _____

2. **AUTHORITY AND LEADERSHIP** (Who are the leaders of Islam, and what authority do they have?)

   _____

   _____

   _____

3. **REVELATION** (How does God communicate with people?)

   _____

   _____

   _____

4. **CELEBRATION** (What are the major holidays, and how are they celebrated?)

   _____

   _____

   _____

5. **SALVATION** (What is "saved," and how do you get there?)

   _____

   _____

   _____

6. **THE MEANING OF LIFE** (What is the purpose of living?)

_____

_____

_____

7. **CORE VALUES** (What are this religion's most important values?)

_____

_____

_____

FATHER AND SON IN PRAYER.
© AYAZAD

Chapter 7.
A Comparison of Judaism and Islam

Muslims have six main beliefs.

- Belief in Allah as the one and only God.

- Belief in angels.

- Belief in the holy books.

- Belief in the Prophets—for example Adam, Ibrahim (Abraham), Musa (Moses), Dawud (David), Isa (Jesus). Mohammad is the final prophet.

- Belief in the Day of Judgment: the day when the life of every human being will be assessed to decide whether he goes to Heaven or Hell.

- Belief in predestination—that Allah has already decided what will happen. Muslims believe that this doesn't stop human beings from making free choices.

Allah

- The heart of faith for all Muslims is obedience to Allah's will.

- There is only one Allah. God has no children, no parents, and no partners. God was not created by a being. There are no equal, superior, or lesser Gods.

- Allah is *eternal*, *omniscient*, and *omnipotent*. Allah has always existed and will always exist. Allah knows everything that can be known. Allah can do anything that can be done.

- Allah has no shape or form; Allah can't be seen. Allah can't be heard. Allah is neither male nor female.

- Allah is just; Allah rewards and punishes fairly. But Allah is also merciful.

- A believer can approach Allah by praying and by reciting the Qu'ran.

- Muslims worship only Allah, because only Allah is worthy of worship.

DRAWN FROM HTTP://WWW.BBC.CO.UK/RELIGION/RELIGIONS/ISLAM/BELIEFS/BELIEFS.SHTML

Maimonides' 13 Principles of Faith

Maimonides was an important Jewish philosopher and teacher who lived and worked as a doctor in the 13th century. He wrote both a major book of law, the *Mishneh Torah,* and a major work of Jewish philopsphy, *The Guide to the Perplexed.* In the book of philosophy he created a list of thirteen important Jewish beliefs. Compare them to the statement of basic Islamic beliefs found above. Circle the ones that match (in both groups). Find the one's that are unique to each religion.

1. I believe with perfect faith that God is the Creator and Ruler of all things. God alone has made, does make, and will make all things.

2. I believe with perfect faith that God is One. There is no unity that is in any way like God. God alone is our God. God was, God is, and God will be.

3. I believe with perfect faith that God does not have a body. Physical concepts do not apply to God. There is nothing whatsoever that resembles God at all.

4. I believe with perfect faith that God is first and last.

5. I believe with perfect faith that it is only proper to pray to God. One may not pray to anyone or anything else.

6. I believe with perfect faith that all the words of the prophets are true.

7. I believe with perfect faith that the prophecy of Moses is absolutely true. He was the chief of all prophets, both before and after him.

8. I believe with perfect faith that the entire Torah that we now have is that which was given to Moses.

9. I believe with perfect faith that this Torah will not be changed, and that there will never be another given by God.

10. I believe with perfect faith that God knows all of people's deeds and thoughts. It is thus written (Psalm 33.15), "God has molded every heart together, God understands what each one does."

11. I believe with perfect faith that God rewards those who keep God's commandments, and punishes those who transgress them.

12. I believe with perfect faith in the coming of the Messiah. However long it takes, I will wait for the Messiah's coming every day.

13. I believe with perfect faith that the dead will be brought back to life when God wills it to happen.

Islamic Belief

WOMAN ENTERING A MOSQUE
IN PENANG, MALAYSIA.
© MARIO SAVOIA

It may sound strange to say this, considering that Islam began in the 7th century C.E., but Islam is the youngest of the great religions we are comparing with Judaism. All of the other religions, including those of the Far Eastern world, had been in business for a very long time before Mohammed came along. As a result, it seems that Islam had the unique opportunity to compare itself and what it taught with all that had come before. (Of course, Christianity could do that with Judaism, but don't forget that most of the very early Christians began as Jews.)

Within the text of the Qu'ran, as you may have already figured out, Islam has much to say about Judaism and Christianity— probably much more about Christianity, because most of the nations that the Muslims conquered were Christian. But as you've also learned, it honored many of the teachings and teachers of Judaism, especially Abraham and Moses. (In fact, Islam explicitly teaches that Abraham was, in fact, a Muslim.) Interestingly enough, it was the Qu'ran that first identified Jews as "the people of the book," although there is some question as to whether that was a good or bad thing. At any rate, one could say that Islam developed many of its ideas in contrast to what had come before, along with Mohammed's own prophecy.

As Islam conquered much of the Middle East, North Africa and Europe, it created a vibrant intellectual civilization while Europe and its Christian leadership were in the Dark Ages. At the same time, as you have read, many Jewish communities flourished under Muslim rule; in part, the difficulties between Israelis and Muslim Arabs is pretty much a creation of the 20th century and the return of our people to the land of Israel. So there has been much exchanging of ideas between our faiths for many centuries—and lucky you, we are about to continue that tradition.

Once again using our basic elements of religions, we will examine how Islam and Judaism compare in those areas where there is significant overlap. Sometimes we might have to say, "Well, we (or they) just don't do that." That's a comparison of sorts, though not in the usual way. So here we go with God and Faith, Authority and Leadership, Celebration and Ritual, and finally, Salvation.

◆ ◆ ◆ ◆

GOD AND FAITH: You will recall *Ilaha illa Allah. Muhammed rasul Allah*, the *Shahada* or great confession of Islam; "There is no God but Allah; Mohammed is the messenger of God." This is roughly comparable in its centrality to our *Shema*: "Hear O Israel, Adonai is our God, Adonai is One." Notice that neither of them are prayers but rather statements of faith in that all-important reality, the Oneness and uniqueness of our own God. The oneness of God is the beginning point of both religions.

Where we differ—substantially I think—is in the issue of transcendence, the idea that "Allah is over and above everything else and therefore cannot really be part of creation as we know it." (That's the definition we used in the last lesson.) Islam says that we can know God's law as revealed to Mohammed, but we can't know God. It's not that Judaism doesn't have such teachings; we do, but they are not the only teachings we have about the nature of God, perhaps not even the prevalent view. One of my favorite Rabbinic sayings about the nature of God is "God is above the world of worlds, and God is also between the hairs of your head." (As I get older I can find much more of God right there on the top of my head.) If you discuss this folksy statement for a while, you will probably decide that it means that God is both "transcendent" and what we call "imminent" or "right near to you, right over there!" That means that God is absolutely everywhere, beyond creation and in creation, and for the most part, that has been the dominant Jewish view over the centuries.

Some people would translate this same idea to say that we believe that God is "personal," but it's more likely that God is "accessible"; we can have a little talk every once in a while. This is reflected in some of the great Jewish philosophers of our tradition, like Tevye the Milkman in "Fiddler on the Roof." Tevye knows that God is above all the worlds, but he talks to the Holy One as if God were standing right there in the barn with him. It is sometimes difficult to argue this idea in philosophy; sometimes it's just a feeling that we have in the way we talk about God and when we communicate with God.

But as Tevye might say, "on the third hand," there are some other things to say about how God communicates with us. In Islam, as you recall (it was only a chapter ago), there is an idea of the uniqueness of Mohammed as God's only prophet, or last prophet. There is a very strong tradition in Rabbinic teaching that still lingers in Jewish philosophy about Moses and the rest of our prophets. The most common statement of this view is "To Moses, God spoke face to face, but to all of the other prophets, God spoke as through a mirrored glass or as in a vision or dream." There was a qualitative difference in the revelation to Moses, and that feeling is held by both very traditional Jews and modern, liberal, even scholarly Jews, who understand that there is a difference in the sacred importance of the Torah of Moses as compared to the other prophetic books such as Isaiah and Jeremiah. (And don't forget that for Christians, Jesus is not a prophet; Jesus is God. So this is primarily an issue for Jews and Muslims.) In this regard, one could say Judaism and Islam agree on the importance of one singular prophet whose experience is critical in the formation of our faiths.

Finally, under the God category, a word about angels as messengers of God. You might be surprised to know that Jewish literature, in the good old days, had a very lively tradition of angels. They have familiar names like Micha'el, Gabriel and even Satan! In some texts they are referred to as God's "familia" (more commonly known as *mishpahah*). There are some angel-like characters in the Torah (the guy who wrestles with Jacob, the figure who appears before Balaam and his donkey), but most of the angel material was written in the Rabbinic period and/or the early Middle Ages. There are named angels in one book of the Bible—Daniel. Some of it did carry over into the mysticism of the later Middle Ages and, nowadays, into the practice of spiritual healing within contemporary Judaism. So once again we find ourselves (although much less so) sharing an idea with the traditions of Islam.

AUTHORITY AND LEADERSHIP: In our earlier discussions about this issue, we talked about such things as authoritative revelation, who wrote the book and who has the power to re-interpret the book, if anybody. On these issues there are very clear differences between Judaism and Islam, and first let's be clear about Judaism. Judaism is essentially a text-based religion, and that text is the Torah. In our stories that Torah is "written" by God and, in some mysterious way or other, given to Moses. But it is very important, and probably news to you, that Judaism has always re-interpreted and expanded the Torah, and those re-interpretations and expansions have been given, especially in the Orthodox communities, the exact same power and authority as the Torah itself.

The thing is that no religion is, or should be, or could be, static, unchanging. The world changes, and the side of us that needs to find meaning and guidance needs new information, new sources of help and hope and understanding. It sometimes happens that ancient texts do not

ISLAMIC WOMAN
WEARING A BLACK VEIL
© RAMZI HACHICHO

103

speak to contemporary needs, even the contemporary needs of two thousand years ago. It sometimes happens that new traditions (that's what we call an oxymoron, like "military intelligence") get created, and they might need to be justified. In Judaism that includes such all-time favorites as the laws of Shabbat and kashrut, medical developments and discoveries that virtually redefine the nature of life and living and your all-time favorite, Havdalah. These things and many others were not included in the Torah of Moses, at least as we know them now. What to do?

Even the Rabbis, of the Talmud understood this problem. So they invented a concept known as Oral Torah. What they wanted to say was that, yes, God gave Moses a Written Torah, but on the side God also whispered a few other minor details in Moses' ear. Then they also said that they, the Rabbis, knew what this Oral Torah contained, and slowly but steadily, they revealed it to us. In actual fact, the Oral Torah is what we know as the books of Mishnah and Talmud, and for traditional Jews these books in which the Rabbis wrote down what was originally oral have the same authority as the Torah of Moses. This is very serious business here, because I think this brilliant concept saved Judaism from becoming irrelevant and impractical and even a little chaotic. This Rabbinic idea opened up the whole world of Torah interpretation and re-interpretation and actually resulted in the creation of brand new laws. The Rabbis tried to base all of their ideas on something that was already in the Torah, but over the centuries Jewish teachers went well beyond that, and authoritative law was created anew. This is, of course, especially true in the liberal branches of contemporary Jewish life.

I am telling you all of this for several reasons. A, it's important; B, it was a good example of the practical brilliance of our Rabbis (so be nice to any rabbis you know); and C, it's a wonderful example of how you learn so much more about Judaism when you study other religions. And what I think is relevant here is that while many Muslim traditions can still function in the modern world, and do, and many individual Muslims live and participate fully in contemporary society, there is a perception that many Muslims, in many Muslim countries, still live in the ancient world and are filled with disdain for the cultural values of the West. Some might say they have not changed or grown as we have. (To tell you the truth, there are still some small sectarian groups within Judaism that think the same thing about other Jews.)

While this is immensely complicated, and even has much to do with the current situation in the world and especially the conflict between Israel and the Arab states, I did promise you that we would stay away from that here. But on the religious difference it is important to note that Judaism has an almost built-in system for change, and I think it is fair to say that Islam has not. And I don't mean to be judgmental about that at all; I think they would agree with this point. Mohammed is the last prophet, and God's revelation to humankind has, for all practical purposes, come to an end. If I may quote one Muslim scholar, "Man does not need new revelations or new prophets. What man needs most is to wake up, to open his mind and to quicken his heart. What he needs now is to make use of the already available Revelation, to utilize his existing resources and to draw from the inexhaustible treasures of Islam, which has incorporated, preserved and perfected the purity of the previous revelations" (Hammudah Abd al 'Ati in *Islam in Focus*). In other words, Islam as presented in the Qu'ran is the right way, and there is no need for internal change for Muslims, or any other belief for other peoples.

CELEBRATION AND RITUAL: This is easy, and we're almost done. If you look at the list of Muslim holidays and their roster of communal celebrations, Islamic celebrations tend to focus on events in the life of Mohammed in much the same way that the major Christian holidays are all about events in the life of Jesus. For all practical purposes, as we have already noted, with the exception of the High Holidays, all Jewish holidays are about events in the life of the Jewish people, all of us. Muslims may have some events of local importance, and of course, there are life-cycle events observing birth and death and everything in between, but the universal celebrations common to all Muslims are all about Mohammed.

SALVATION: This is also pretty easy. Islam, as you read, has rather expansive definitions of Heaven and Hell. But if you caught my drift, the point of these details, they teach, is to make you behave in this world so that when the time comes you get resurrected and you get to go to Heaven instead of you-know-where. There is a Day of Judgment on which this decision is reached. So I guess you could answer the Salvation question—i.e., "What is that we are saved from?"—with "You are saved from going to you-know-where."

Here comes another place where through studying other religions you get to learn something more about Judaism.

We have already talked about the fact that Judaism answers the salvation question through the concept of changing the world and saving it and us from the horrors of injustice. That's the real deal, and it's who we are and what we seriously believe. But just for fun (well, not that much fun), you might be interested to know that in traditional Jewish sources there are two concepts floating around known as the *Olam ha-Ba* and *Gilgul ha-Nishamot*. The first is "the world to come" and the second is literally "the rolling around of souls," or what some might call a kind of reincarnation. There are also, just for serious fun (another oxymoron), some sources about a final judgment day and a resurrection of the dead.

What I would like us to think about, since they have at one time or another crept into the popular imagination of the Jewish people, is why they have and why, from time to time, they still do. All religions, from time to time, with varying degrees of importance, have incorporated these concepts, and since we're comparing us with them, we might as well understand why they get in.

THE OPENING PAGE OF A QU'RAN MADE IN ISTANBUL IN 1867 C.E.

© KAZUYOSHI NOMACHI/ CORBIS

I think it's mostly because from time to time, people need them. They are, at their core, about the certainty of death and what that means for the purpose and meaningfulness of life. People are afraid of dying, and it's nice to know that in some way or other life could go on. It's comforting. Some of these concepts are about another of life's worries. What if you're good and you never get rewarded or noticed for your goodness? Well, God notices, and since God is around forever, God can guarantee you that you'll get rewarded in some forever kind of place. It doesn't really matter how far away that forever place is; the eternal God will always be there to make sure you're there, too. And of course, as Muslim teachers have said, some of these are just stories to make you behave. On the other hand, if they're more than just stories—if they're true and you didn't behave—aren't you in for a nasty surprise? And sometimes, as with the idea of the reincarnation of souls, these teachings are attempts to explain the often mysterious things that pop up in our world, like when we think we used to be a butterfly. So don't be surprised if every once in a while you find some Jewish stories about ideas that you used to think belonged only to the Christian and Islamic ideas of Heaven and Hell. Every once in a while we did it, too.

◆　◆　◆　◆

Now that we have finished our comparison of Judaism and Islam, I'll bet you're surprised to have discovered that we do have many things in common—at least more than you might have thought when we began. But clearly, as we have often said, there are some other issues that divide Jews and certain Muslims in our world today. We have seen that at least some of this happened because zealous Muslims in the early stages of Islam's development emphasized the conversionary and militant verses of the Qu'ran, and some are doing it again. And some of it is happening because of social and political issues in the Middle East and has nothing to do with religious principles. All of this is why I hope you will feel that there is much about Islam to admire and respect, and why I hope we all feel that we can find some way to peacefully resolve the other issues that divide us.

Exercise

Here is one text from the Qu'ran and one from the Bible. Compare them.

INTERIOR OF THE BLUE MOSQUE— SULTANAHMET MOSQUE
© ERIC ISSELÉE

> Successful indeed are the believers, those who humble themselves in their prayers, who avoid vain talk, who are giving *zakat* (charity), who guard their modesty, except with those joined to them in the marriage bond, or the captives whom their right hands possess, for in their case they are free from blame.
>
> But those whose desires exceed these limits are transgressors. Those who faithfully observe their trusts and their covenants, and who strictly guard their prayers...those will be the heirs who will inherit Paradise. They will dwell there forever. (Qu'ran, Sura 18, vv. 1-11)

Psalm 1 Happy is the person who has not followed the advice of the wicked, nor stood together with sinners, nor sat in the seat of the scornful. But such a person's delight is in the law of the Eternal; and on God's law meditates day and night...For the Eternal cares about the way of the righteous; but the way of the wicked shall perish.

How are they similar? How are they different?

_____

_____

_____

109

The Five Pillars of Islam

The "five pillars" are the core of Muslim practice. Write down a Jewish practice that is similar to each one.

1) Faith: There is no god worthy of worship except God, and Muhammad is God's messenger. This declaration of faith is called the *Shahada*.

_____

_____

2) Prayer: *Salat* is the name for the required prayers that are performed five times a day. The prayers are led by a learned person and contain verses from the Qu'ran. Prayers are said at dawn, noon, mid-afternoon, sunset and nightfall. Although it is preferable to worship in a mosque, a Muslim may pray almost anywhere.

A translation of the Call to Prayer is:

> *God* is most great. *God* is most great.
> *God* is most great. *God* is most great.
> I testify that there is no god except *God*.
> I testify that there is no god except *God*.
> I testify that Mohammad is the messenger of *God*.
> I testify that Mohammad is the messenger of *God*.
> Come to prayer! Come to prayer!
> Come to success (in this life and the Hereafter)!
> Come to success!
> *God* is most great. *God* is most great.
> There is no god except *God*.

> *Compare this to the* בָּרְכוּ *Barekhu, the Jewish call to worship.*

_____

_____

3) The *Zakat*: The word *zakat* means both "purification" and "growth" but is the equivalent of the Hebrew *tzedakah*, "charity" (righteous giving). Our possessions are purified by setting aside a portion for those in need. Like the pruning of plants, this cutting back balances and encourages new growth. Each Muslim calculates his or her own *zakat* individually. For most purposes this involves the payment each year of two and a half percent of one's wealth. The Prophet said: "Charity is a necessity for every Muslim." He was asked: "What if a person has nothing?" The Prophet replied: "One should work with his own hands for personal benefit and then give something out of the earnings in charity." The Companions asked: "What if he is not able to work?" The Prophet said: "One should help poor and needy persons." The Companions further asked "What if one cannot do even that?" The Prophet said "One should urge others to do good." The Companions said, "What if one lacks that also?" The Prophet said, "One should keep from doing evil. That is also charity."

_____

_____

4) **The Fast: Every year in the month of Ramadan Muslims fast from first light until sundown, abstaining from food, drink, and sexual relations.** Those who are sick, elderly, or on a journey, and women who are pregnant or nursing are permitted to break the fast and make up an equal number of days later in the year. If one is physically unable to do this, one must feed a needy person for every day missed. Children begin to fast from puberty, although many start earlier. Even though the fast is beneficial to health, it is regarded principally as a method of self-purification. By cutting oneself off from worldly comforts a fasting person gains true sympathy with those who go hungry as spiritual growth.

_____

_____

5) **Pilgrimage (*Hajj*): The annual pilgrimage to Makkah (Mecca).** About two million people go to Makkah each year from all over the world. Pilgrims wear special clothes: simple garments which strip away distinctions of class and culture, so that all stand equal before God. The rites of the Hajj, which are of Abrahamic origin, include circling the *Ka'ba* (black stone) seven times, and going seven times between the mountains of Safa and Marwa as did Hagar during her search for water. Then the pilgrims stand together on the wide plain of Arafa and join in prayers for God's forgiveness, in what is often thought of as a preview of the Last Judgment. The close of the Hajj is marked by a festival, the *Eid al-Adha*, that is celebrated with prayers and the exchange of gifts.

_____

_____

Chapter 8.
Welcome to the East

Judaism and the Eastern Religions

Here are two texts. One of them is Buddhist, and one of them is Hindu. Based on whatever you know (1) read them both; (2) find the differences between them; (3) then, if you can, make a guess as to which is which.

Text 1

Whatever takes form is false.
Only the formless endures.

When you understand
The truth of this teaching,
You will not be born again.

For God is infinite,
Within the body and without,

Like a mirror,
And the image in a mirror.

As the air is everywhere,
Flowing around a pot
And filling it,
So God is everywhere,
Filling all things
And flowing through them forever.

(Ashtavakra Gita 1:18-20)

Text 2

The greatest achievement is selflessness.

The greatest worth is self-mastery.

The greatest quality is seeking to serve others.

The greatest precept is continual awareness.

The greatest medicine is the emptiness of everything.

The greatest action is not conforming with the world's ways.

The greatest magic is transmuting the passions.

The greatest generosity is non–attachment.

The greatest goodness is a peaceful mind.

The greatest patience is humility.

The greatest effort is not concerned with results.

The greatest meditation is a mind that lets go.

The greatest wisdom is seeing through appearances. (*Atisha Bassui*)

_____

_____

_____

_____

East May Be Midwest

AN OLD RELIGIOUS MAN
FROM INDIA

© THEBAND

In the United States and North America, when you learn all the stuff that you're supposed to learn you sometimes get your sense about the rest of the world a little misdirected. Everything else is where it is in relation to where we are. On top of that, sometimes our geography is mixed up with our politics. Europe, for example, because it's part of what we call Western Civilization, is still considered the West even though it's to our East. Israel and her neighbors, however, are called the Middle East, though they should probably be called the Near East since they're so near to Europe. At the other end of the East is what we call the Far East (China, Japan, etc.), even though it's pretty near to our West Coast. Put India, Pakistan, Afghanistan and their neighbors into all of that, and perhaps they're the real Middle East. It's really confusing!

Much of this happened, I suppose, because we think we're the center of the universe and everything should be located in terms of where it is from us. But of course, the point is that we're not the center of the universe, and the religious traditions that we will be studying from the East all developed well before the United States ever showed up. At their formation they never knew about East and West; they just knew what was important and valued in their lives. So let's be sure that we study these faiths with an appropriate and respectful perspective; no matter where they come from, they have lessons to teach that have endured a very long time.

We're about to study what we call the Eastern religions; well, actually, two of the Eastern religions. Mostly they come from, or grew up in, countries like India, Japan, Tibet and thereabouts. But if we use the term Eastern in the broadest geographical sense, then Judaism, Christianity and Islam also began as Eastern religions. Christianity and Judaism both *moved* to what we might call the West and over many centuries both religions influenced Western culture and, in turn, were influenced and profoundly changed by Western cultural and social values. Some would even say that they *became* Western in nature; they became the religions of Western civilization. Islam, in its early history, *conquered* some of Western Europe but then was forced to retreat back to the Middle East and North Africa. Only in recent history have large numbers of Muslims begun to appear in the West and engaged in different forms of relationships with Western culture, though not all of them are what we would call "religious".

The Eastern religions, relatively speaking, are a new experience for us; it's only been for one hundred years or so that we have learned to "look to the East." We are still getting acquainted with religious experiences that are very different from anything we have seen in the West. In fact, unlike Islam, our relationship with it would seem that much of our initial contact with Eastern religion has been focused on religious expression. For example, many scholars will argue that the meditative experiences that are rapidly growing within liberal Judaism are in response to what we have learned about them from the Eastern religions. Judaism does have an ancient meditative tradition within its mystical Kabbalistic teachings, but one could argue that we only dusted them off and reopened their wisdom in response to what our contacts with Buddhism, for example, have awakened within us. Religions do interact and influence one another, and sometimes that interaction produces change and novelty; and sometimes that change and novelty produces both gain and loss at the same time.

For all practical purposes, Eastern religions are those that developed and flourished in the vast and varied lands of Asia—countries like India, China, Japan, Tibet, Korea, Vietnam, Russia and many more. We are going to concentrate on Hinduism and Buddhism because they are the most widespread and because they are the ones you will most likely encounter in some form in North America and/or other parts of the so-called West. We're also going to examine Buddhism particularly carefully, because there are a lot of committed Jews who engage in common Buddhist practices. They have actually formed a sort of subculture within American Judaism referred to as "Bu-Jews."

Some of the other religions of the so-called East of which you may have heard include Taoism, Confucianism and Shinto. I'll bet you're wondering what happened to Zen; don't worry, it's actually a part of Buddhism, but we're not going to learn anything here about maintenance of your motorcycle. (Just in case you're not getting that, there was a book published not too long ago called *Zen and the Art of Motorcycle Maintenance.* I have no idea what that was about.) But first, let's see what Hinduism is about and how it may compare with Judaism.

Hinduism

Hinduism is one of the oldest religions in the world; in fact, it may be the oldest among the active religions in the world today. Unfortunately, its origins are lost in antiquity, and it's not possible to establish an exact date for its origin. We do know for sure that Hinduism originated in northern India, near the Indus River (are you seeing some language connections here?), at least four thousand years ago. It's a lot different nowadays, but then again, what or who isn't? One of the reasons that it is so different today is that so many other religious ideas from other sources were added to the original teachings of Hinduism. Eventually these ideas were synthesized into the body of the Hindu faith, but many scholars will say that Hindu is not just one religion, but a collection of many different religions blended into one. Perhaps that's why it can be a little difficult to grasp.

Over this long history, most Hindus were in India, and Hindu beliefs and practices have had a profound effect on the culture of India itself. India is a Hindu country in the same way that many countries are Muslim and Israel is Jewish. Today Hinduism is practiced by more than 80% of India's population. But as Indians, like so many others, have begun to settle in other lands, Hinduism has gone along with them for the journey. It is currently the third largest religion in the world, with about 750 million followers. That's a lot of karma, and that was your first somewhat-sneaky introduction to a Hindu concept that you probably have heard about; but you'll have to wait a little while to find out exactly what it is.

About God

Scholars and religious historians (most of whom are also scholars) tell us that Hinduism has no founder like Moses or Jesus or Mohammed. It grew out of an even more ancient philosophy that we can call Brahminism. Brahman (not to be confused with Brahm,s who composed one of the lullabies your parents may have sung to you) is more or less the "universal soul" of the world, a

COLORFUL HINDU WOMEN BATHING IN THE GANGES IN VARANASI
© REGIEN PAASSEN

single God. But to confuse matters just a little bit, Brahman takes on many different forms in the world, and various Hindus worship those various forms as their "immediate" God, something they can relate to and about which they tell stories from which they learn values and beliefs and customs.

While Brahman is the creator of the world, a god named Vishnu is its Preserver, and Shiva is its Destroyer. Shiva is married, and Mrs. Shiva goes by four different names or roles. As Parvati or Uma she is the beloved goddess of motherhood. But as Durga or Kali she is the feared goddess of destruction. Hindus believe, in a rather realistic way of looking at the world, that these contrasts in Mrs. Shiva actually represent the way in which the world works, moving from birth to death and from creation to destruction. It is valuable to recognize these contrasts, and belief in these contrasting god-figures gives Hindus a place where they can find comfort and understanding.

Along with this really complicated list of gods (there are more), Hindus believe that because Brahman (the soul of the universe) is in all things, animals also have souls, just like us. As a result, Hindus worship some gods that appear in the form of animals, and you may have heard that in India cows are sacred. (You may also have heard that sometimes here in America we have a lot of things that we call "sacred cows," and we don't always mean it in the best of ways, but it is a term we borrowed from India.) Along with cows, some Hindus also worship monkeys and snakes. Yes, snakes!

About Authority and Literature

As with other religions, Hinduism has a vast written history that has changed and developed over its very long life. The oldest are known as the *Vedas,* and there are four of these Books of Knowledge. They come from a time when early Hindus were touched by the wonder of nature and existence, but they range over a wide variety of topics about the world, about appropriate behavior and the nature of Brahman. They also contain hymns and prayers and some of the basic theology of Hinduism.

The other sacred scriptures of Hinduism are the *Upanishads,* the *Smrutis, Ramayana, Mahabharta* and the *Puranas.* Much of the material in these later books contains stories of the Hindu heroes and some of the various gods. The *Upanishads* contain the first reference to one of Hinduism's biggest ideas, that of reincarnation and karma. In these other books you can find descriptions of basic Hindu rituals, and in the *Mahabharta* you can read one of the most famous and powerful poems in world literature, the *Bhagavad-Gita* (the Song of God), the story of a war between two branches of a family. All of these books are written in Sanskrit, the original language of India.

Needless to say, this literature is the basic authority of Hinduism, and over the centuries it has been carefully taught and analyzed and discussed by the teachers and priests of Hinduism. The greatest authorities are those who have been revered for their knowledge of this basic literature, for their personal practice and wisdom and for their saintly, heroic deeds. You actually know who some of these people are, in a way. Some of these saints are known as **YOGIS** (but not the famous catcher for the Yankees. Believe me, there is no way that Yogi Berra practiced yoga, though I wouldn't be too sure about Yogi Bear), and some of the great teachers are called **GURUS**. These familiar terms tell us that what was once so far away and long ago is now a part of our lives, too.

Hindu worship, where all this is studied and practiced, happens every day at home, where many families maintain a personal shrine. These shrines often contain a representative statue of one of the different forms of God. Communal worship takes place at a **MANDIR**, or temple, which is dedicated to a god. At the temple Hindu worshippers bring offerings of water, fruit, flowers and incense to the god in charge. The liturgy is referred to as a **MANTRA** (I'll bet you've heard that word before, too), during which they repeat the names of their favorite gods and/or goddesses.

Two Other Really Big Ideas

Hinduism has contributed two other major concepts to the culture of India, to Hindu followers, and in many respects, to the rest of the world. There are other ideas, too, but let's concentrate on these two major thoughts that are involved with our task of comparing religions. One of them is the idea of reincarnation, which is how it is that Hindus deal with the question of what we have called "salvation." The other idea is that of the caste system, and it speaks to our study of how people live together in their religious communities. It is a unique idea that is very different from what we know in Western religions and Western civilization.

SAMSARA (Reincarnation) and **KARMA**: Because of the Hindu belief that the soul never dies even if the body does, the Hindu faith teaches that after your physical death the soul is reborn in another state, most often higher or lower than the previous one. It's not that you move from California to Illinois, but you may move to another human body, or perhaps even that of an animal or a plant. Where your soul winds up depends on how you did in the life that just ended. This process is continuous and is known as "reincarnation"; and how well you do, or don't do, depends upon what is known as *karma*. The law of *karma* says that every action has an influence upon how the soul will be born in the next reincarnation. When your friends tell you that you must have good or bad *karma*, it means that something from your past life is having an influence on how you're doing in this one.

However, the process is not really endlessly continuous. If you're really good, there may come a time when you achieve what is called **MOKSHA**, when you or your soul is released from the cycle of reincarnation and you unite with Brahman, the universal soul.

This would roughly be the equivalent of what we have come to talk about as "salvation." The more that you do the good stuff, the sooner you can achieve *moksha*. The "good stuff" includes following the **DHARMA**, the Hindu code for a moral and pure life; the pursuit of spiritual knowledge through meditation and yoga; and serious work for the good of the society

WOMAN MAKING
OFFERING TO THE GODS
AT VARANASI, INDIA
© JEREMYRICHARDS

in which you live. This pursuit of *moksha* in which you build up your karma is summed up in what Hinduism refers to as the paths of knowledge, meditation, devotion and good works.

THE CASTE SYSTEM: The social structure of Hindu communities, especially in India, is perhaps their most distinctive characteristic and one that Western cultures can find difficult to understand. Society is divided into four different groups or "castes," each of which has its own group of rules that must be followed. You are born into one of these four specific castes (and there are often sub-castes within them), and you cannot change from one to another. Only good karma earned during that particular life of your soul can elevate you to another caste—or, as you might guess, bad karma can send you the other way—unless you're really bad and you wind up as an animal or a plant.

Hindu religious law maintains strict separation of the castes at almost all levels of existence, from occupation to marriage and all sorts of personal contact. This has begun to change in modern India, especially in the cities, but its influence is still present throughout the country, where members of different castes are very strictly separated. The highest caste is that of the Brahmans, the priests and scholars. Next are the rulers and warriors, followed by the merchants and professionals and lastly the laborers and servants. A vast group of people often called the "untouchables" is completely outside of the caste system, and for years these people suffered greatly in Indian society. But in the 1950s the government of India actually banned what was referred to as "untouchability," and for all practical and legal purposes, discrimination against such people has disappeared. As modernism has developed in India, individuals from different castes who would never have mixed or worked together or married now interact quite frequently and easily. It's another example, as in all religions, of the effect that modern life has had on ancient cultures.

OLD MAN PERFORMING ABLUTION AT JAMA MASJID, DELHI, INDIA

© SALAMANDERMAN

Comparing Hinduism and Judaism

By now, after all this study of various religions, you should be pretty good at figuring out the similarities and differences between them and Judaism.

So it should be pretty clear that the Hindu concept of God is partly the same and partly very different. Brahman is a god of universal significance, and it would not be un-Jewish to use such a phrase or concept as "the soul of the universe" to describe various Jewish ideas of God. On the third hand (as Tevye would say), Judaism has never accepted the notion of physical representation of God in various personalities or physical manifestations. In a very strict interpretation of traditional Jewish law, the representation of God in any physical manner, such as in the statues and paintings of Hinduism, would be idolatry. But that's what makes for different teams on the baseball fields of life.

As you might also have guessed, the vast literature of Hindu history and religious teaching is pretty much what all religions have as the source and authority of their teachings. Every religious group has its own Torah, but it is of course a different story with vastly different content.

Samsara (reincarnation) and *karma* do raise some interesting issues for us. Judaism also believes that the soul, the breath of God, is eternal. How could the breath of God not be? But we also believe that over the years of our life, our soul becomes forever intertwined with the persona of our own life, with us as individuals and the choices we make. For the most part, Judaism teaches that your soul is your soul and will not become that of someone or something else. On the other hand, this might be a good time to take a brief look at the Kabbalistic concept of *Gilgul ha-N'shamot*, more or less translated as "the rolling around of souls." (Maybe you remember a Hebrew song about railroad trains rolling along on their *galgalim*, their wheels.)

This idea was very popular among the Jewish mystics of the late Middle Ages and early modern centuries. In twenty-five words or less, it taught that if a soul had unfinished business, it just might find its way into another life; and in fact, depending on the nature of that other business, it could do better or worse. One of my favorite examples of this idea is in a commentary by the great scholar Nahmanidies on the biblical book of Job. Job is a difficult and challenging piece of literature, and it tells a most remarkable story. Job suffers devastating punishments from God because of a bet God makes with Satan. God is convinced that Job, a righteous man, will not abandon his beliefs despite these absolutely undeserved tragedies. Nahmanidies and the Kabbalists, in an attempt to explain why God would do this, invoke the principle of *Gilgul ha-N'shamot* to say that within Job there was the reincarnated soul of another person who apparently, had not been as righteous as Job appeared to be. It was that person that God was punishing. and that person clearly had some bad *karma*.

INSIDE HINDU TEMPLE ON BALI ISLAND.
© DMITRY RUKHLENKO

This concept is still studied and debated within Kabbalistic communities and from time to time comes up in many different contexts—sort of a "maybe" thing when nothing else will explain what's going on. It never became a part of mainstream Jewish thought, but we should not deny that it is a part of our religious history.

Finally, Judaism has, of course, never had anything like a caste system. We do, however, have an extensive history and lots of legal literature about the process of excommunication, of officially declaring people guilty of certain sins to be outside the community. It's certainly not a social structure in the manner of the four major castes, but in the history of its implementation there is a ring of "untouchability" in what happens to the person who is excommunicated. It doesn't happen too much anymore, and if you do your homework, it won't happen to you, either. There have been some recent (relatively speaking) famous examples of excommunication, one of them in Cincinnati when a famous Orthodox rabbi declared all of the Reform Jews of Cincinnati to be in *Herem*, the Hebrew term for excommunication. So here again we find some unexpected sort-of-similarities between Hinduism and parts of Jewish life.

Exercise

There are six texts about Hinduism on pages 125 and 126. Three are traditional. Three are by famous people. Write the "big idea" that each text is expressing. Pick a favorite.

Text 1

We are the birds of the same nest,
We may wear different skins,
We may speak different languages,
We may believe in different religions,
We may belong to different cultures,
Yet we share the same home—
OUR EARTH.

Born on the same planet
Covered by the same skies
Gazing at the same stars
Breathing the same air
We must learn to happily progress
together
Or miserably perish together,
For man can live individually,
But can survive only collectively

(Atharva Veda)

A HINDU MONK PERFORMS A MORNING PUJA IN VARANASI.
© KAZUYOSHI NOMACHI/CORBIS

Big Idea _____

_____

Text 2

A king asked a sage to explain the Truth. In response the sage asked the king how he would convey the taste of a mango to someone who had never eaten anything sweet. No matter how hard the king tried, he could not adequately describe the flavor of the fruit, and in frustration he demanded of the sage "Tell me, then, how would you describe it?" The sage picked up a mango and handed it to the king, saying, "This is very sweet. Try eating it!" *(Unknown)*

Big Idea _____

_____

125

Text 3

Where there is separateness, one sees another, smells another, tastes another, speaks to another, hears another, touches another, thinks of another, knows another. But where there is unity, one without a second, that is the world of Brahman. This is the supreme goal of life, the supreme treasure, the supreme joy. Those who do not seek this supreme goal live on but a fraction of this joy. *(The Upanishads)*

Big Idea_____

_____

Text 4

When I read the *Bhagavad-Gita* and reflect about how God created this universe everything else seems so superfluous. *(Albert Einstein)*

Big Idea_____

_____

Text 5

When doubts haunt me, when disappointments stare me in the face, and I see not one ray of hope on the horizon, I turn to the *Bhagavad-Gita* and find a verse to comfort me; and I immediately begin to smile in the midst of overwhelming sorrow. Those who meditate on the *Gita* will derive fresh joy and new meanings from it every day. *(Mahatma Gandhi)*

Big Idea_____

_____

Text 6

In the morning I bathe my intellect in the stupendous and cosmogonal philosophy of the *Bhagavad-Gita*, in comparison with which ourt modern world and its literature seem puny and trivial. *(Henry David Thoreau)*

Big Idea_____

_____

Basic Hinduism

To conclude, use this chapter and fill in the following categories.

1. **GOD AND FAITH** (Who is the God and what are you supposed to believe?)

   _____

   _____

   _____

2. **AUTHORITY AND LEADERSHIP** (Who are the leaders of Hinduism, and what authority do they have?)

   _____

   _____

   _____

3. **REVELATION** (How does God communicate with people?)

   _____

   _____

   _____

4. **CELEBRATION** (What are the major holidays, and how are they celebrated?)

   _____

   _____

   _____

5. **SALVATION** (What is "saved," and how do you get there?)

   _____

   _____

   _____

6. **THE MEANING OF LIFE** (What is the purpose of living?)

_____

_____

_____

7. **CORE VALUES** (What are this religion's most important values?)

_____

_____

DEEPAVALI CELEBRATION MALAYSIA
© SYAMSUL BAHRI MUHAMMAD

Chapter 9.
And Now...on to Buddhism...

Here are five short Buddhist parables. Based on them, what can you say about Buddhism as a religion?

Holding on to anger is like grasping a hot coal with the intent of throwing it at someone else; you are the one who gets burned. *(Gautam Buddha)*

Three things cannot be long hidden: the sun, the moon, and the truth. *(Gautam Buddha)*

If you live the sacred and despise the ordinary, you are still bobbing in the ocean of delusion. *(Lin-Chi)*

JAPAN, KAMAKURA, GREAT BUDDHA STATUE
© ANYAIVANOVA

We're all in this together—by ourselves. *(Lily Tomlin)*

A flower falls, even though we love it; and a weed grows, even though we do not love it. *(Dogen)*

_____

_____

_____

_____

_____

Buddhism Is Different

Before we begin to look at Buddhism in depth, there is an important introductory word—actually several words—to say. At the end of it all we will find that Judaism and Buddhism have virtually no major ideas that are incompatible with one another. Buddhism looks as if it has many of the major elements of religions that we have discussed, but at its core it is more about a system of behaviors that help you reach certain understandings about your place in the world. You could even say that Buddhism does not have a god in the classical sense of the word, and its many customs and ceremonies are sort of a lifestyle. So this section will look a little different than some of our other sections, and that should become apparent to you as you study.

BUDDHA HAND AND HEAD.
© LUCIANO MORTULA

Buddhism is named after its first teacher and founder, referred to as the **BUDDHA**. The word "Buddha" is from the language of Sanskrit, common to ancient India, where the Buddha was born around 560 B.C.E. (at about the same time the Israelites were living in exile in Babylonia). His real name was Siddhartha Gautama, and he was the son of King Suddhodana and Queen Mahamaya, the rulers of a small kingdom within what is now Northern India. The title "Buddha" is from the Sanskrit verb *budh*, "to awaken," and it is usually translated as "Awakened One Supremely Awakened." His title has nothing to do with a good nap during religious school, but it has everything to do with the principal teachings of Buddhism.

As with Christianity and Islam, the primary text of Buddhism tells the life story of the Buddha and the teachings that developed from his life experience. Those teachings became known as the **DHARMA** (the word means "truth"), and we'll learn more

130

about them later. He taught the dharma to a community of followers who promised to follow the same kind of life that the Buddha did, a simple life of meditation and teaching in which they sought the truth. We would call them "monks"; in Sanskrit they are called **ARBATS**. These monks formed monasteries (places where monks live) that attracted many more followers, and in time, large numbers of people came to know and love the teachings and stories of the Buddha.

AN OLD BUDDHIST JOKE: What did the Buddhist say to the hot dog vendor? "Make me one with everything!"

None of this was written down in any organized way for quite some time, mostly because people in those days had much better memories than we do. Finally, in the 3rd century B.C.E., in a language known as Pali, in the land of Ceylon (now called Sri Lanka), a "canonized" (authoritative and official) text of the *dharma* was written. It is called the **TRIPITAKA**, the Three Baskets, because it organizes the stories and teachings of the Buddha into three distinctive subject areas. However, they're not super-organized; they are anthologies and anecdotes. There is no single author, but rather they represent the collected recollections that more or less official councils gathered. Now let us gather together to see what is the *dharma* of the Buddha.

The Dharma of the Buddha

The core of the Buddha's teaching is very simple and is directly related to his life story. If you remember, the word or name "Buddha" has to do with being awakened, and Buddhism, more or less, is about how we become awakened and to what it is that we become awakened. The Buddha was awakened, and then he went and told everyone else about it and suggested ways in which they could achieve the same goal. In the simplest terms, we are awakened to ourselves, to our fullest possibility as humans and to the oneness of the world in which we live. There are things that get in the way of realizing all of that, and the Buddha's teachings are about the methods with which you can awaken from the stuff that gets in the way and find the real world. (And what is especially important for you to recognize now, I bet, is that the vocabulary of this idea doesn't sound too strange to you. These ideas are not necessarily central within the religions we have looked at so far, but it should be obvious that they have gotten pretty far into the world in which you live.)

Here's what happened to the Buddha. His father, the king, wanted to shield his son from the difficulties of the world and so kept him within the walls of the palace. For the first part of his life he was trained in all of the requirements of a warrior king. He was a great athlete; he became more skilled than all of his teachers. He was also kind and compassionate and an absolute whiz at math and literature. He found a beautiful bride; one legend has it that he met her when he won an athletic competition. He had a wonderful life, but he also sensed that he was missing something, and he longed to see the world outside of the palace walls. The king reluctantly agreed, but even so, he tried to control all of the things that Siddhartha would see. Fortunately, he failed; otherwise we'd have no Buddhism!

Through a series of events the Buddha discovered that not all the world was as perfect as his childhood had been. Illness and pain and death, all kinds of suffering, were just as much a part of reality as the pleasure he had known. Suffering, he concluded, was inevitable, and he really didn't know what to do. Somewhere along the way he met a monk whose tranquility and serenity lead the Buddha to believe that there must be some way to find peace within a world that knew so much pain. He needed to find the truth—a kind of spiritual truth about the way the world really was and how you could understand it and live with it. And so he renounced everything he had, shaved his head, put off his royal garments and set off to meditate in the wild forests of India.

He went to the wild forests because apparently there were many "truth seekers" already working the woods. But none of them could teach him anything that helped, no matter how many different extremes he tried. And he tried them all, including barely eating anything and/or meditating himself into near-unconsciousness. He finally decided that he had to get healthy in order to see a little more clearly. Eventually he decided that extremism and self-denial were not the answers, and it led him to the idea of what came to be called **THE MIDDLE WAY**, the first important teaching of Buddhism. This simple yet difficult-to-achieve goal means that one shouldn't get too attached to one side or the other.

BUDDHIST RITUAL IN CHINA
© YANFEI SUN

All things in the world are interrelated, and it is a mistake to try to divide them, good vs. evil, self vs. others, mind vs. body, all or nothing. Find the mean to be serene. (The Buddha didn't say that; I just threw in a little interpretive free verse.)

Once he got his head and body clear, it wasn't long before he got into the really big stuff of Buddhism, the real enlightenment that helped him to understand and live in the real world. As he calmly looked at the world around him, he saw that everything was interconnected and interdependent (for example, just think about your relationship with air and water and plants and sun). No one can escape from the intricate web of life. On top of that, he learned that nothing is permanent, and therefore each moment is precious. The impermanence of everything means that we and everything else are going to die; therefore suffering and loss are inevitable. We yearn for things we can never have, but once we realize and accept that, we are a part of the reality of the world. We can moderate our expectations and live at peace. He was enlightened, he was fully awake, he was Buddha.

After all this time in the woods, the Buddha realized he had an obligation to teach these ideas to the rest of the neighborhood. And so he organized his lectures, developed a system of meditative techniques and outlined the principles that would be the stuff of our meditation. These big ideas of Buddhism would become known as **THE FOUR NOBLE TRUTHS** that define the origins of suffering and the liberation from it, and **THE EIGHTFOLD PATH**, the program by which you can get all this done. He decided to call these teachings the *dharma*, the truth or the path, and for the remainder of his life he went all over his world with what he had discovered. So let's get with the program!

◆ ◆ ◆ ◆

The Four Truths (as defined by Karen Armstrong, the noted scholar of world religions, in her biography of the Buddha) are pretty clearly derived from the life story of the Buddha:

1. Life is difficult.

2. Life is difficult because of attachment, because we crave satisfaction in ways that are inherently dissatisfying.

3. The possibility of liberation from difficulties exists for everyone.

4. The way to realize this liberation and enlightenment is by leading a compassionate life of virtue, wisdom and meditation. These three spiritual "trainings" (virtue, wisdom and meditation) comprise the teachings of The Eightfold Path to Enlightenment.

You should understand that this is not a judgment about whether or not the world is a good or bad place. It is meant to be a simple description of the way things are; it's meant to be realistic, not optimistic or pessimistic. *Don't let it get you down.* That's just the way it is, and with a little work you can get around it and find happiness.

The way to find enlightenment (a much more refined state of being than happiness) is through The Eightfold Path, the training routine of wisdom, ethics and meditation—the discipline that gets to where you need to be. Different scholars and interpreters of the Buddha's ideas may use slightly different words for each of these steps, but it should be pretty easy to figure out how they work toward the ultimate goal of enlightenment. They are usually portrayed as a circle with spokes rather than a straight line through which you progress from one to the other. This can get a little complicated, for what the Buddha meant by this idea is that sometimes you will want to connect a couple of the steps. Karen Armstrong divides the eight steps into three groups, as you will see here.

WISDOM TRAINING

> Step 1: Right View (which, of course, you got once you understood the Four Truths)
>
> Step 2: Right Intentions (Plan to do the right thing)

ETHICS TRAINING (Conducting yourself in a really good way)

> Step 3: Right Speech
>
> Step 4: Right Action
>
> Step 5: Right Livelihood

MEDITATION TRAINING

> Step 6: Right Effort (trying really hard, breathing deeply, easily)
>
> Step 7: Right Mindfulness (paying attention to what you're doing, and only what you're doing)
>
> Step 8: Right Concentration (getting the *dharma* deep into yourself)

Not everybody writes these out this way (and the parenthetical statements are mine), but perhaps with a little discussion you can see how each of these fits within its title virtue. This is, of course, much more involved than these simple sentences, but for now I hope you will simply see them as the **CORE VALUES**, the essential elements of Buddhist teaching and practice.

got too much into the idea of the Oneness of all things. We certainly got into the idea of the Oneness of God, but don't confuse the two. For most of the Jewish way of thinking, God remains mysterious and hidden and awesome, not at all common, not in all things. There has to be a difference between the created world and the Creator; and even though we often say that the world is sacred, that is simply because we believe that God had something to do with its creation and with the way things work within the created world. Certainly some things in the world are extraordinary, but that doesn't necessarily mean that God resides within them. Human beings are created in the image of God, and Judaism teaches that our soul is a "breath of God" within us, but we are certainly not God, no matter what your grandmother says about you.

What Is Zen, Anyway?

ZEN STONES
© OLGA
LYUBKINA

There is, of course, a great deal more to Buddhism than this very simple and brief introduction. There are specific teachings about how to meditate; there are many different traditions within the many different lands in which Buddhism is observed. You may have questions about all those statues of the Buddha, and what exactly is **ZEN**, anyway? *Zen* is a school of Mahayana Buddhism notable for its emphasis on practice and experimental wisdom—particularly as realized in the form of meditation known as *zazen*—in the attainment of awakening. There are special recipes and foods that contribute to the quality of life, and there are the unique chants and melodies of Buddhist traditions. We haven't even mentioned celebrations and holidays, and—isn't it interesting?—there seems to be no mention of God within the stories and teachings of the Buddha. For many people, Buddhist practice seems to be an antidote to the pressures and stress of Western civilization, and there is a whole cultural world of Buddhist art and music and dance to help them. What does the average day of an observant Buddhist look like? What does an average Buddhist look like?

You may have the opportunity to explore some of those questions, but the only other issue we are going to look at here is our basic challenge to compare religions. And when it comes to Judaism and Buddhism, as we have said, that task is relatively simple. For all practical purposes, it seems to me that there is nothing contrary to Judaism in Buddhist teaching. Maybe that's why there are so many Bu-Jews! While (as we have read) Judaism has a minor meditative tradition, there is no reason why the meditative techniques and goals of Buddhism would be prohibited to us. There is much spiritual and practical wisdom within Buddhism that could easily complement and enhance what Jews believe and do. On the other hand, Buddhism neither emphasizes nor contradicts what is uniquely important to Judaism: peoplehood, Torah study, the covenant with God, social justice and community. The relationship between Judaism and Buddhism is perhaps as close to apples and oranges as we have gotten. It's almost a fruit salad!

Buddhist Texts for Jews to Choose

Once more you have three Buddhist texts. Read them. Find the big idea that each one is teaching. Pick your favorite.

The thought manifests as the word;
The word manifests as the deed;
The deed develops into habit;
And habit hardens into character,
So watch the thought and its ways with care,
And let it spring from love
Born out of concern for all beings...
As the shadow follows the body,
As we think, so we become. *(From the Dhammapada, The Sayings of the Buddha)*

_____

When sitting, sit like a Buddha. Be Buddha.
When standing, stand like a Buddha. Be Buddha.
When walking, walk like a Buddha. Be Buddha.
When thinking, think like a Buddha. Let Buddha think through you.
When breathing, breathe like a Buddha. Let Buddha breathe through you.
Let Buddha live through you. Be Buddha.
Enjoy the natural great perfection.
You are far more Buddha-like than you think. *(Source unknown)*

_____

THE FIVE REMEMBRANCES: A BUDDHIST MEDITATION

1. There is no way to escape aging. I too will grow old.

2. There is no way to escape physical degeneration. My body too will weaken.

3. There is no way to escape death. I too will die.

4. Everything and everyone changes, we must part even from loved ones.

5. My deeds are always with me as propensities. Only my karma accompanies me when I die; my karma is the ground on which I stand.

_____

Karma is a Hindu idea, but Buddhists who lived in the same geographic neighborhood managed to pick it up and use it in their own way.

What are some of the ways that Buddhism and Judaism fit together?

_____

_____

What problems are there for a Jew looking at Buddhist wisdom?

_____

_____

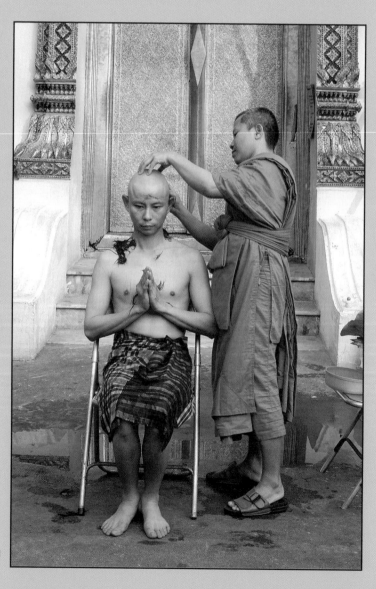

THAI MAN GETS HIS HEAD
SHAVED BY A MONK DURING
A BUDDHIST ORDINATION
CEREMONY.

© GINA SMITH

138

Basic Buddhism

To conclude, use this chapter and fill in the following categories:

1. **GOD AND FAITH** (Who is the God, and what are you supposed to believe?)

   _____

   _____

   _____

2. **AUTHORITY AND LEADERSHIP** (Who are the leaders of Buddhism, and what authority do they have?)

   _____

   _____

   _____

3. **REVELATION** (How is truth revealed to people?)

   _____

   _____

   _____

4. **CELEBRATION** (What are the major holidays and how are they celebrated?)

   _____

   _____

   _____

5. **SALVATION** (What is "saved," and how do you get there?)

   _____

   _____

   _____

6. **THE MEANING OF LIFE** (What is the purpose of living)?

_____

_____

_____

7. **CORE VALUES** (What are this religion's most important values?)

_____

_____

BELL AND DORJE, TIBETAN BUDDHISM SYMBOLS
© BARTOSZ OSTROWSKI